The Real Economy of Zaire

The Real

THE CONTRIBUTION OF SMUGGLING

Economy

& OTHER UNOFFICIAL ACTIVITIES

# of Zaire

TO NATIONAL WEALTH

Janet MacGaffey
with
Vwakyanakazi Mukohya
Rukarangira wa Nkera
Brooke Grundfest Schoepf
Makwala ma Mavambu ye Beda
Walu Engundu

upp University of Pennsylvania Press
PHILADELPHIA

University of Pennsylvania Press
Blockley Hall, 13th Floor, 418 Service Drive, Philadelphia,
Pennsylvania 19104-6097

First' published 1991

Library of Congress Cataloging-in-Publication Data
MacGaffey, Janet.
    The real economy of Zaire : an anthropological study / Janet MacGaffey, with
Vwakyanakazi Mukohya . . . [et al.].
        p.   cm.
    Includes bibliographical references (p.   ) and index.
    ISBN 0-8122-3140-6 (cloth). — ISBN 0-8122-1365-3 (pbk.)
    1. Economic anthropology — Zaire.   2. Informal sector (Economics) —
Zaire.   3. Economics — Zaire — History.   4. Zaire — Commerce.   5. Zaire —
Economic conditions.   6. Zaire — Politics and government.
I. Title.
GN654.M25   1991
306.3'096751 — dc20   91-3844
                                                                          CIP

ISBN 0-8122-3140-6 (cloth)
ISBN 0-8122-1365-3 (paper)

Typeset in 11/12 pt Palatino by Colset Pte Ltd, Singapore
Printed and bound in Britain
by Villiers Publications, London N6

Contents

Tables, Maps & Figures

Acronyms

ANEZA	Association Nationale des Entreprises Zairoises
BAT	British American Tobacco
BEAU	Bureau d'Etudes, d'Aménagement et d'Urbanisme
CECOPANE	Centre de Commercialisation des Produits Agricoles du Nord-Est
ECOWAS	Economic Community of West African States
GECAMINES	Général de Carrières et des Mines du Zaire
MPR	Mouvement Populaire de la Révolution
OFIDA	Office des Douanes et Accises
ONPTZ	Office National des Postes et Télécommunications du Zaire
OZAC	Office Zairois de Contrôle
OZACAF	Office Zairois du Café
UNTZA	Union National des Travailleurs Zairois

Note

The unit of currency is the zaire (Z) divided into 100 *makuta*.
In March 1987, 100Z = $US 1

1 hectare (ha) = 2.47 acres

Acknowledgements

The authors gratefully acknowledge the help and contributions of many people at different times in the preparation of this book; in particular, at the inception of the study to Franco Fornasari and Adriana DeLeva. For the carrying out of the research we owe an immeasurable debt to all our Zairian informants and to Professor Makwala's research assistants and supervisors. We would like to thank Lee Cassanelli for his constructive suggestions for revision, Claude Schoepf for his critical comments on and patient assistance in preparing the manuscript of chapters 4 and 6, and Cynthia Yaudes for correcting and preparing the final manuscript for the press. Most especially, we are grateful to Jean-Marie Cour for his ideas, and to Wyatt MacGaffey and Tom Callaghy for their critical comments and discussion of the chapters by Janet MacGaffey.

The Authors

Janet MacGaffey, Assistant Professor of Anthropology, Bucknell University, Lewisburg, Pennsylvania.

Vwakyanakazi Mukohya, Professor of Anthropology, National University of Zaire, Lubumbashi, Zaire.

Rukarangira wa Nkera, Co-Director, Project CONNAISIDA, Kinshasa, 1986–88; Takemie Fellow, Harvard School of Public Health, 1989–90; Consultant, WHO Global Program on Aids, 1989–

Brooke Grundfest Schoepf, Director, Project CONNAISIDA, Kinshasa, 1986–1990; Evelyn Green Fellow in the Social Sciences, The Bunting Institute, Radcliffe College, Harvard University, 1989–90.

Makwala ma Mavambu ye Beda, Professor of Anthropology, National University of Zaire, Kinshasa, Zaire.

Walu Engundu, Chef de Section, Stratégies de Survie des Femmes, Centre de Recherches en Sciences Humaines, Kinshasa; Fellow, Women and Development Program, Institute of Social Studies, The Hague, 1990–91.

Introduction
JANET MACGAFFEY

In most countries of the world, alternative economic systems known variously as informal, underground, parallel, unrecorded or second economies exist alongside official ones. In socialist societies, the rigidity of central planning and control has given rise to alternative forms of production and distribution outside the state system; in developed capitalist societies, moonlighting, tax evasion, fiddles and perks, and barter pervade the workplace; in developing societies, the spiralling decline of the official economy is often offset by flourishing activities unreported in the national accounts. The phenomenon is so widespread, so large in scale, and so well integrated into the functioning of almost all economies that it is the subject of considerable concern to tax authorities, government policy planners, and development agencies; it poses a challenge to many economic assumptions and has profound implications for policy formulation.

The primary problem with this state of affairs is that conventional economic analysis ignores this ever-expanding sector of the total economy because it does not appear in official reports and statistics. The increasing extent of unofficial economic activities is amply documented in the press and in scholarly journals. It is becoming a matter of considerable urgency worldwide to formulate new approaches to the study of national economies which can include these activities instead of focusing only on the ever-diminishing fraction of the total economy represented by the official economy.

One such new approach formulates the concept of the 'real economy', which covers the totality of all economic activity and moves beyond the limitations of the narrow range of activities that are reflected in the national accounts of the official economy. This approach provides the context and framework for this book. The data presented here focus primarily on the unrecorded trade of Zaire's second economy, but we want to raise a larger issue. If assessments of the economy of any country are to be realistic, it is essential that they comprise the entirety of economic activity. In our documentation of smuggling and unlicensed trade in Zaire, the vast flow of commodities unmeasured by the national accounts makes

1

very clear the importance of looking at the real economy rather than only at the official one. Zaire is not unique in Africa in this respect.

Our smuggling data reveal that the second and official economies do not form distinct sectors of the real economy, but are interlinked in many complex ways: the same individuals participate in both, a commodity may pass between the two in the course of successive transactions, unofficial and official modes of importing may be combined at all stages of the journey. Consequently the phenomena with which we are concerned are as much political and social as they are economic. Knowledge of them is as necessary to policy makers, planners, and aid organizations as to academics. In particular, this study offers, firstly, a new and realistic perspective to bring to bear on the economic and political situation of other countries of the continent as well as Zaire. Secondly, it documents the limitations to the liberalizing reforms of the World Bank and the IMF, showing in specific detail how their implementation is limited by political, infrastructural, technical and socio-cultural factors at the local level.

Although the scale of the second economy in different countries is documented in a few full-scale studies by economists, in a number of journal articles and in newspaper reports, little is known about its causes and consequences, organization, profits and expenses, the factors that motivate people to participate in it, or the precise nature of its linkages with the official economy. Such information is lacking because not only is this part of the total economy unrecorded and unmeasured, but many of its activities are covert and on the other side of the law and thus difficult to investigate.

Anthropologists are peculiarly suited to investigate a topic of this kind. They are accustomed to dealing with societies lacking statistics, in which economic transactions take place in the context of personal relationships, and they carry out research by developing personal contacts and relations of trust with informants. The authors of this book are all anthropologists. They present qualitative data to complement the quantitative work of economists on alternative economies and to advance our knowledge of an increasingly significant phenomenon on which precise information is urgently needed.

The book grew out of a three-month collaborative research project organised by Janet MacGaffey in the spring of 1987. The aim of the project was a systematic comparative study of unrecorded trade in three border regions of Zaire and a household study in Kinshasa. Vwakyanakazi Mukohya, Makwala ma Mavambu ye Beda, Rukarangira wa Nkera and Walu Engundu carried out this project. Subsequently, Brooke Schoepf, who has done extensive research, lived, and taught in Zaire, joined the group in writing the book, contributing insights from some of her own research and data from ongoing projects on which she is working with Rukarangira and Walu.

Four of the authors are citizens of Zaire. The contacts, local knowledge

2

and unique insight of these Zairian scholars have made it possible to provide information on clandestine activities that would simply not be available to foreign researchers. Their extraordinarily valuable data was, nevertheless, collected in conditions of considerable difficulty and in a short period of time; it represents a remarkable achievement. Vwakyana- kazi Mukohya studied unrecorded import and export in North Kivu; Rukarangira wa Nkera investigated unrecorded trade within Southeast Shaba and with Zambia and other countries; Makwala ma Mavambu ye Beda's study of unlicensed trade between Kinshasa and Luozi zone in Lower Zaire includes research on smuggling to the Republic of the Congo; and Walu Engundu's data from eighteen households in Kinshasa docu- ments incomes and expenditures to show just how much money is needed to live in town. She makes clear the essential role of women's trade in household maintenance.

All four Zairian researchers, despite being local to the regions studied, found the research very arduous because of the often illegal nature of the activities being investigated and because of the logistical difficulties in doing research in Zaire, such as transportation and communication pro- blems, rising prices and therefore research costs, and the endless delays that beset any endeavor in the current political and economic situation. Vwakyanakazi writes of breakdowns in bus services in Kivu because of broken bridges; Rukarangira recounts how he had to ride a bicycle for a day and a half along narrow paths in the bush, and make long journeys on top of an open truck over appallingly bad roads; Mak- wala reports delays in his project because of the difficulty of getting money to his research assistants working in the villages; and Walu needed extraordinary persistence to persuade women traders who were, with good reason, very guarded about their affairs, to allow her continually to visit, observe and record their activities.

Part I of the book gives an overview of the issues and a general discussion of Zaire's second economy. It is divided into two chapters. The first outlines the theories and ideas on alternative economies, expounds the concept of the 'real economy', addresses the question of the extent to which Zaire is unique in the nature of its second economy, and reflects on the policy implications of the findings of this study for Zaire and for African countries in general. The second chapter gives some background material on Zaire, then focuses on Zaire's unrecorded trade, exploring its cultural and structural dimensions. Part II is made up of the four regional studies: three on cross-border and rural-urban trade; the fourth on women's trade and how households make ends meet in Kinshasa, to show how far the earnings of illicit trade reported in the other studies can go in terms of spending power. The book ends with a brief concluding chapter, assessing the consequences, both negative and positive, of the second economy, and the nature of the transformation it has brought about in Zairian society.

3

I OVERVIEW

1 Issues and Methods in the Study of African Economies
JANET MACGAFFEY

A New Approach to Evaluating Economic Reality

Officially the economy of Zaire is in a state of disaster: exports cannot keep up with imports, production lags, industry barely functions, scarcities are rife, the infrastructure has deteriorated drastically, wages are at starvation level and nothing works as it should. But the reality on the ground is that, despite the severe economic crisis, a population of 35 million people, which is also the third largest in terms of urban population in sub-Saharan Africa, finds the means to survive, with some people thriving and becoming wealthy.

Clearly, the true picture is not reflected in the national accounts and official economic reports: a great deal of economic activity is taking place outside the official system. It is through these unofficial activities that the economy really works; instead of looking at the official economy we should therefore be looking at the unofficial one. What has previously been thought of as a marginal sector of the economy is, in fact, the principal means by which it operates. What is needed is a new conceptual framework for looking at the real state of the economy, at the totality and not just its component parts; we will propose a means to do this. Our study of unofficial activities focuses on the magnitude, organization and motivation of unrecorded trade within Zaire and across its borders. Comparison with other African countries shows that Zaire is not unique in either the size or form of its unofficial economy, and that, realistically, African economies need to be considered in multi-country regional studies as well as in studies of individual nations. The chapter will end by suggesting some policy implications arising from this approach.

We will begin with some definitions and conceptualizations of various categories of economic activities taking place outside the official system. Unofficial economic activities have been referred to in various terms. To the terms informal, underground, parallel, unrecorded and second, we can add hidden, shadow, endogenous, irregular, alternative, unofficial, or

7

black economy. The term 'second economy' is used here on the grounds that it is preferable to 'underground' or 'hidden', because many of its activities are carried out quite openly; preferable to 'parallel', because unofficial activities intersect with official ones in many complex ways; preferable to 'informal', because this term has come to refer to the small-scale enterprises of the urban poor, ignoring large-scale activity of much greater significance for the national accounts; and preferable to 'unrecorded' because the word is too neutral and does not have the connotation of illegality that is an essential element in the political implications of this sector of the economy.

We should note here that indigenous terms exist for this phenomenon. In Ghana, it is *kalabule*; in Uganda, *magendo*; in Angola, *candonga*. People in Zaire refer to *l'économie de débrouillardise*, or *système D*, or say simply: '*Nous vivons mystèrieusement*', for which the meaning is unambiguous.

Concepts and Definitions in Historical Perspective

Keith Hart first drew attention to informal income opportunities outside the formal wage economy. In Accra, Ghana, he found that people solved the problem of the inadequacy of urban wages by holding more than one job or by engaging in petty enterprises of all types, ranging from small to large in scale, often in addition to wage employment. 'Denied success by the formal opportunity structure, these members of the urban sub-proletariat seek informal means of increasing their incomes' (Hart 1973: 67).

In distinguishing between formal and informal income opportunities, 'the key variable is the degree of rationalization of work – that is to say, whether or not labour is recruited on a permanent and regular basis for fixed rewards' (ibid: 68). This distinction derives from Weber's theory that economic progress is inhibited by irregularity and unpredictability in social life. For Weber, the rational/legal state was the guarantor of emergent corporate capitalism in a process leading to increasing formality in economic organization. From this point of view, Third World states are seeking to establish hegemony over their economically backward populations. Much economic activity, however, is only marginally the product of state regulation and is in this sense 'informal' relative to the forms of publicly organized economic life. This is a qualitative distinction; neither size nor productivity can be intrinsic to the definition of informal enterprises (Hart, 1985: 56). This formulation of Hart's is ignored in much literature on the informal sector, which is often defined in terms of size of enterprise and type of production, despite the difficulty and inconsistency involved. Hart is also careful to point out that the term 'informal sector' refers to activities or roles and not to persons (Hart 1973: 66). The same

8

individual often operates on both sides of the analytical divide, even in the course of a single transaction.

The pervasiveness and size of these second economies everywhere indicate that figures on employment and unemployment bear little relationship to the realities of earning an income. Hart shows that wage incomes are only part of the urban opportunity structure: 'We need not think all of those who enter informal occupations do so as a result of failure to obtain a wage-job. The magnetic force of the town may be derived from the multiplicity of income opportunities rather than merely from wage levels' (Hart 1973: 88). The data in this study reveal the wide range of alternatives to wage employment by which people manage to live in Zaire today.

Hart's concept of the informal economy was taken up by policy makers, development agencies and researchers. Whether its effects were considered to be good or bad varied according to ideological conviction. The perspective taken by political economists such as Portes and Walton, for example, is pessimistic and negative (Portes and Walton 1981). The informal economy is held to subsidize the large firms of the formal economy both directly and indirectly: as a source of cheap goods and services for their labor force it allows them to pay extremely low wages. From this viewpoint the informal economy is exploitative and repressive. Those taking this approach sometimes define this economy in terms of petty commodity production (for example, Moser 1978).

The positive liberal perspective, exemplified by the ILO, sees the informal economy as creating employment and producing goods and services for low-income groups. It is seen as relatively autonomous, with a vitality that gives it a potential for expansion. Governments are pressured to make policies that reduce constraints on informal economy enterprises so as to absorb the unemployed. The informal sector is supposed to further development because it is less capital-intensive and less dependent on foreign exchange and technology than the formal economy. Optimists see in informal activities 'the possibility of a dramatic 'bootstrap' operation, of people improving underdeveloped economies through their own indigenous enterprise' (Hart 1973: 88). They are seen as an 'endogenous economy' rooted in and growing from within society.

Both these views neglect the political dynamics that help to explain the scale and expansion of second economies.[1] The second economy exists for political as much as for economic reasons; its activities are supposedly under the control of the state but either evade this control or involve illegal use of state position. It is important to see them not simply as solutions to household survival or individual subsistence problems, but rather as political options, co-opted by political discourse (Redclift and Mingione 1985: 4). What is legal or illegal varies from country to country and also

9

over time as policies change. Government intervention does not create informal practices but changes the context in which they take place and their legal definition. The margin between the legal and the illegal, the legitimate and the illegitimate is often shadowy. Ultimately it is the responsibility of the state to define legitimate economic activity and enforce its definition (*Outer Circle Policy Unit* 1976: 1–2). The state, however, operates to further the interests of the dominant class. Through the second economy, the citizenry may not only evade civil obligations but also express resistance to the state and to the class which controls it.

Marxists see only the repressive aspects of this economy and fail to see that unofficial activities can also offer opportunities for enrichment and social mobility, and that they have the potential to affect the process of class formation (as I have argued elsewhere: MacGaffey 1987; MacGaffey 1991). Liberal optimism, on the other hand, does not sufficiently take harsh political realities and constraints into account. These political dynamics are responsible for the difficulty researchers have had in identifying and defining the unit of study for investigations of the 'informal sector'. To avoid this difficulty a new conceptual framework is needed that includes all economic activity, instead of dividing it up arbitrarily and unrealistically.

The Real Economy

Since official statistics are so misleading, we need to adopt a different approach and address economic issues from a global perspective. Such a perspective has been developed by economist-demographer Jean-Marie Cour, a Senior Economist at the World Bank.[2] It encompasses all components of economic activity, all transactions monetized and non-monetized, official and unofficial, taking place between rural and urban areas of a country, to arrive at a picture of the total economy, which is the 'real economy'. Despite the fact that the data presented here chiefly concern unrecorded trade of various kinds, within Zaire and across its borders, this concept is the broader issue that we wish to emphasize. The real economy consists of: the recorded economy, that is, all economic activities that are recordable and reported and that are gathered by statistics; the non-monetized economy, that is, all activities concerned with non-monetized production for self-consumption; and all the remainder, which is monetized (though operating with a variety of currencies and also through barter), unrecorded and, because it is more or less illegal, inadmissible. It is this last which we call the second economy.

According to Cour, a social accounting matrix is the most practical means for assessing the real economy. The starting point is household

10

expenditure. Production can be concealed, but consumption is traceable through expenditures. The first step is to establish a matrix of population distribution, to analyse the population by type of settlement and by main way of living, or dominant activity, and to identify categories of households accordingly. In Zaire, population statistics and household expenditure figures are more reliable than figures on other aspects of the economy. Expenditures of each category of household and the sensitivity of these expenditure patterns to changes in the macro-environment can be compiled. A social accounting matrix can show how the incomings and outgoings of each category of household, institution, commodity and activity balance. It must include all real and financial flows corresponding to monetized and non-monetized production, consumption, transfers, savings and investments.

The value of the social accounting matrix is that the data on income and outgo must balance not only within each of three dimensions, the sectorial, the spatial and the social, but between dimensions. The sectorial dimension, with the economist's usual input-output analysis relating production to consumption, can be re-analysed in spatial terms to show the flow of economic activity between urban and rural areas, between and within regions, and in relation to the local distribution of the population. Lastly, the same global or real economy can be analysed in social terms, dividing the population into its significant sectors: small farmers, wage workers and business owners, civil servants, political elite, and others.

The several analytical dimensions of the matrix demand, and find places for, data obtainable from a variety of sources. Data on private expenditure according to category of household can be derived from household surveys and interviewing. Public sector accounts provide data on public expenditure, together with estimates of unrecorded production of public goods and services from local government and other organizations, and from field studies such as those presented here, describing economic activities and transactions that may not be readily quantifiable.

Estimates made through such calculations show that the real economy of Zaire may well be as much as three times the size of the official GDP. Economic estimates arrived at by this method are certainly more likely to reflect economic realities than are official statistics. The gross inaccuracy of such statistics for developing countries has been graphically demonstrated by Polly Hill (1986). Her definitive critique emphasizes the value of an anthropological approach, of small-scale, more accurate, qualitative studies. The aim of this book is to provide qualitative, detailed and localized data on a category of economic activities, an extremely significant part of the economy, which official statistics gatherers do not incorporate into the national accounts.

11

The context of our study then, is the real, or total, economy of Zaire. The second economy is an integral part of the real economy. Investigating it will yield more valuable information on how the economy really works than will conventional economic perspectives based on faulty and incomplete statistics. The reader should keep in mind the importance of considering the total economy of any country while we look at the unrecorded trade that is the primary focus of the book. We will look now at the reasons for the rapid expansion of the second economy of Zaire in the last fifteen years.

The Second Economy: Causes and Underlying Circumstances

Some scholars have defined what we are calling the second economy in a very broad sense, as all unreported and unmeasured economic activity falling outside the scope of a nation's technique for monitoring the economy (Feige 1979), or all income-producing activities outside the official wage and social security system (Portes 1981: 87). These definitions include the household and subsistence economy. Ours is narrower. The second economy is here defined as economic activities that are unmeasured, unrecorded and, in varying degrees, illegal. They consist of: i) legal production of goods and services concealed to avoid taxes or other charges; ii) production of illegal goods and services; iii) concealed income in kind, which includes the profits of barter; iv) other income opportunities that are illegal or in some way deprive the state of revenue. These categories separate criminal illegal activities from activities that are legal in themselves but illegal in that they evade taxes or in some other way deprive the state of revenue.

Using this definition we are following several other writers who find it important to distinguish between activities that are merely unmeasured and those that are concealed in order to evade taxation or licensing and other regulations (Smith 1985: 6–8; Mattera 1985: 4–14; Blades 1982: 30–33; Gershuny and Pahl 1980: 7). Peter Wiles, in particular, uses 'illegitimate' as the overarching word for the second economy (Wiles 1987: 21–22). The populace breaks state laws and regulations which they reject as unacceptable. As Anne Witte emphasises: 'The essence of the underground economy lies in the relationship between the government and economic activity. An underground economy can only exist if there is a formal economy' (Witte 1987: 79). It is 'the people's spontaneous and creative response to the state's incapacity to satisfy the basic needs of the impoverished masses' (De Soto 1989: xiv). Herein lies its political aspect.

The economic context of the expansion of the second economy in Zaire in the seventies and eighties is of falling world market prices for principal export commodities and also of the heavy burden of increasing national debt. This situation has resulted in severe shortages of foreign exchange for essential and luxury imports, the functioning of industry far below capacity, and the decay of the infrastructure. The transportation system, in particular, has grossly deteriorated. Vehicles, railway stock, river boats and ferries cannot be adequately maintained because of shortages of spare parts and fuel; many roads, especially in the rural areas and regions remote from the capital, have become unusable for lack of funds and spare parts for maintenance equipment. As a result of this situation, scarcities of goods are rife, foreign exchange for importing is officially unobtainable for all but a powerful few, and the official marketing system barely functions. As people take matters into their own hands, seeking to find remedies for these problems, the second economy has expanded.

The quadrupling of oil prices in the seventies played a part in the expansion of second economies worldwide. Pierre Péan suggests that corruption escalated globally and changed its nature as a result of this severe price rise. According to Péan, western bankers discovered that the way to profit from petrodollars was to lend them to the rulers of the Third World. Commercial interests then converged upon these elites and sold them expensive development projects on an immense scale so that they became heavily indebted. Many of these supposed development projects were simply opportunities for corruption as intermediaries demanded commissions. Rulers thus diverted funds and enriched themselves while their people starved (Péan 1988: 9-12).

All of these factors have contributed to the recent rapid expansion of the second economy in Zaire, but its most important underlying cause has been extremely low wages relative to prices, a situation that has been chronic throughout the colonial and post-colonial periods but which has markedly increased in severity throughout the seventies and eighties.

In this period, the real purchasing power of incomes declined sharply: in 1983 public service salaries were nominally seven times higher than in 1975, but in real terms they represented less than one-fifth of the 1975 level. In relation to 1969, prices were 46 times higher in 1979, and 113 times higher in 1986 (Houyoux et al. 1986: 10). In 1984, the National Institute of Statistics (INS) estimated that an average monthly food budget for a family of six was 3,037 Z, while the base monthly salary for a *medium-level civil servant was 750 Z*. Despite salary increases (in 1984, 1986 and 1987) a reduction in personal income tax, and non-salary benefits in the private sector accounting for over 60% of a worker's compensation package, wages still fall drastically short of providing for minimum living requirements, especially for the bulk of the labor force who are employed at lower wage levels. But only about one million of the estimated four-million labor force is employed and earns any wage in the official economy at all. Urban dwellers must thus find outside the formal wage and salary system not only the sole means for survival if unemployed, but also essential supplementary income if they are employed, as well as income for any improvements in living standards or for becoming wealthy. Given these circumstances,

13

the fact that the urban population does survive, feed, clothe and house itself, with varying degrees of difficulty or prosperity, is a significant indicator of the enormous size of the second economy and of the much greater dynamism of the real economy than is apparent in the national accounts.

We can find some specific indication of what this situation means at the level of individual lives. A 1986 survey of household incomes and expenditures in Kinshasa shows how much larger was actual income, calculated from expenditures, than income from salaries. Average incomes were as follows (in zaires):

	Salary	Income	Income as % of Salary
Managers	6,949	20,797	299
Salaried workers	4,469	10,578	237
Skilled labor	2,720	7,397	271
Semi-skilled labor	2,797	6,046	216
Unskilled labor	2,331	4,993	214

(Income is calculated from consumption and also transfer expenditures, such as repayment of loans, gifts, savings, rotating credit payments)

Source: Houyoux et al. (1986: 35)

On average, in all households in the survey, only 25% of income came from wages and salaries, 29% came from unknown sources, primarily illicit and described as '*Je me débrouille* (I get by)', and the rest came from gifts, rents, savings, etc. (ibid: 36–37).

In the same year, a study of food consumption in Zaire's major cities showed that 67.4% of monthly household expenditures in Kinshasa went on food (BEAU, 1986). The average amount spent was 5,314 Z, a figure that is astonishing when compared with the salary levels given above. Kinshasa's population has increased from 901,000 in 1967, to 1,636,000 in 1975, and to 3,000,000 in 1986 (Houyoux et al. 1986: 1). Household size increased at the same time from 4.8 persons in 1967, to 5.72 in 1975, and to 7.33 in 1986 (ibid: 57). The serious decline in spending power in this period is reflected in the increasing consumption of cereals and decreasing consumption of protein in the form of fish and meat (ibid: 11).

An important consequence of this huge gap between wages and salaries and the income necessary for even a modest standard of living, is that the first and most time-consuming activity of officials at all levels of the bureaucracy is, initially, actually to get their wages, because often they are simply not paid, and then somehow, to increase them by some five to twenty per cent. Since all but the lowest-level administrative officials are regularly rotated between posts in different regions, most of them do not have the opportunity to develop any economic enterprise but must rely instead on the power of their office for extortion in the form of personally-levied taxation on services that as part of their jobs should be provided free. All this obviously detracts from the effectiveness and quality of public administration.

A question that arises from this exposition of the enormous size and continuous expansion of Zaire's second economy is: to what extent is this situation peculiar to Zaire?

How Unique is Zaire?

Zaire is not unusual in the size of its second economy. For example, in Uganda *magendo*, the black market economy, is estimated at two thirds of, or even to exceed the GDP (Green 1981; Prunier 1983: 62). According to Alphonse Kayombe, an official at the Central African Republic's Banque Centrale, illicit trading operations represent 75% of the country's national budget (Schissel 1989: 43). In Morocco, the size of the black market economy is estimated to be about one third of reported GDP, or over $6 billion a year (ibid). A conservative estimate in Tanzania is that on average about 30% of economic activity is not accounted for in the official statistics and takes place in the second economy (Maliyamkono and Bagachwa, 1990: 61).

Nor is Zaire unique in the gross inadequacy of wages and salaries relative to prices. In Ghana, in early 1980, a minimum wage earner, if he received his pay at all, could buy only a staple starch for his family for one week. In Conakry, Guinea, in 1985, salaries supplied on average only 10% of household income. This meant that on his pay an official could only feed his family for the first three days of the month. Employment became important not for the money it could bring but for the social capital it represented: jobs brought access to the profitable opportunities of a parallel commercial system developing in the heart of the state. Profits were invested in real-estate and commerce, accentuating the speculative and inflationary tendencies of the economy (Morice 1987). In Uganda in 1980, a modest middle-class standard of living in Kampala required a pre-tax income of 200,000 to 250,000 shillings a month, but a senior civil servant received a salary of only about 75,000 shillings (Green 1981). By 1988, the minimum monthly wage of 1,500 shillings (less than $10 at the official rate of exchange and $3 on the black market) bought one-and-a-half bunches of bananas, the staple food (*Christian Science Monitor* Dec. 29, 1988). In Angola, neither workers nor high-ranking officials can support their families on their official earnings. A few purchases on the parallel market in 1985 used up a whole month's wages: one egg cost half a day's

15

salary for a worker; the price of a chicken was the equivalent of six days' salary for an official (Morice 1985: 113–118). In Tanzania, an average household of six can feed itself on formal wages for only four to six days of the month; a minimum of 80% of household income comes from income other than wages (Tripp 1988: 6). This is over two-and-a-half times the figure cited above for Kinshasa.

The press and scholarly journals also continuously report throughout Africa the large-scale clandestine trade across national boundaries of food and export crops, of essential and luxury manufactured goods, of precious minerals and ivory. Zaire is certainly not unique in this respect either. In 1980 four-fifths of cocoa production was smuggled from the Volta region of Ghana to Togo or left unharvested, and in the seventies and early eighties smugglers exported 12–15% of Ghanaian gold and diamond production (Chazan 1982: 18). In 1985, the smuggling trade accounted for export of two-thirds of Senegal's peanut crop to Gambia, and a highly organized illegal trade in medicines, arms and drugs flourished (Fassin 1986). In Sierra Leone, diamond smuggling exports an estimated two-thirds of annual production (Legum 1983–84: B580); according to sources close to the diamond industry, losses may amount to between $50 to $60 million of revenue annually (Momoh 1988). In Angola, official diamond exports dropped from 1.5 million carats in 1980 to 1.03 in 1983 because of smuggling (Legum 1983–84: B612). Diamang, the Angolan diamond company, is reported to be losing as much as 50% of its revenue to smugglers (*Southern African Economist* 1, 6: 12). Coffee and gold are smuggled out of Uganda on a huge scale (Green 1981). Cameroon lost an estimated 85 billion CFA francs in customs dues because of the smuggling trade to Nigeria of food crops in return for manufactured goods (Fodouop 1988: 24).

Price distortions across frontiers often influence such trade. They enabled smugglers to sell Ghanaian cocoa for three to six times as much in neighboring countries as in Ghana in 1978 (Jeffries 1982: 4). The subsidized price of gasoline in Guinea in the eighties meant that it could be sold on the black market for ten times as much in Senegal as in Guinea (Morice 1987). Government subsidies for food production in Zambia make smuggling profitable for the higher prices for the same foods offered in Zaire; as much as one-third of the Zambian maize crop illegally crosses the border.[3]

This extensive illicit movement of commodities is governed by: the natural resources available locally; geographical location; the factors governing supply and demand, both internal and external to the countries involved; political and economic conditions in neighboring countries; and local and national transportation conditions.

There are some respects in which Zaire does seem to be unique, principally in its specific historical circumstances and the form of state and society that have resulted.[4] The power of the Belgian 'colonial trinity' of

16

state, church and big companies; the lack of education, management skills and experience among Zairians; and an economy intended to export primary materials at the expense of food production; all these were factors in the political and economic problems, both short and long term, that followed upon the sudden granting of independence in 1960. These problems were compounded by ethnic division and conflict. Mobutu restored stability, centralizing the state after he seized power in 1965, but reckless public spending, a disastrous indigenization process and the decline in world commodity prices contributed to the deepening economic crisis into which Zaire has spiralled since the mid-seventies.

Apart from its particular historical circumstances, Zaire is set apart in Africa to some degree by the limitless pursuit of wealth by the powerful clique that runs the country. It is also perhaps unique in the nature of its state. So ineffective is the Zairian state in terms of administrative efficiency, judicial function and provision of public services, that some writers have expressed doubts of its continuing existence (Newbury 1984; Young 1984). But although it does not perform these usual functions of a state, nor uphold the civil rights of its citizens, it nevertheless functions most effectively to further the interests of the clique that controls it. The secret police and its network of informers is highly organized and effective in stifling any opposition to the regime. The state monopolizes force and the army and gendarmerie are brutal coercive tools (Callaghy 1984; Schatzberg 1988). Furthermore, position in the state can offer access to the second economy, to the allocation of scarce goods and resources, to foreign exchange, and to opportunity for extortion and corruption of all kinds. The higher the position the more lucrative the possibilities. We have already shown how the low pay of civil servants and the way they are moved around is a major factor in this situation.

Zaire is certainly unique in its immense natural resources, though its regions are not all equally well endowed (Map 1.1), and in its strategic location in the heart of Africa: its frontiers all border regions diverse in commercial opportunities. Although Zaire is not unique in having massive flows of clandestine trade across its borders, the length of its frontiers and the variety of economies to which they give access does perhaps give a particular advantage in such trade. Some estimates of the quantity of commodities smuggled across Zaire's borders will show how fully Zairians exploit this advantage.

The Massive Scale of Zairian Smuggling

The state loses enormous amounts of revenue from smuggling and fraudulent export of the primary products that are a principal source of its revenues. Since the seventies, from 30–60% of the coffee crop

17

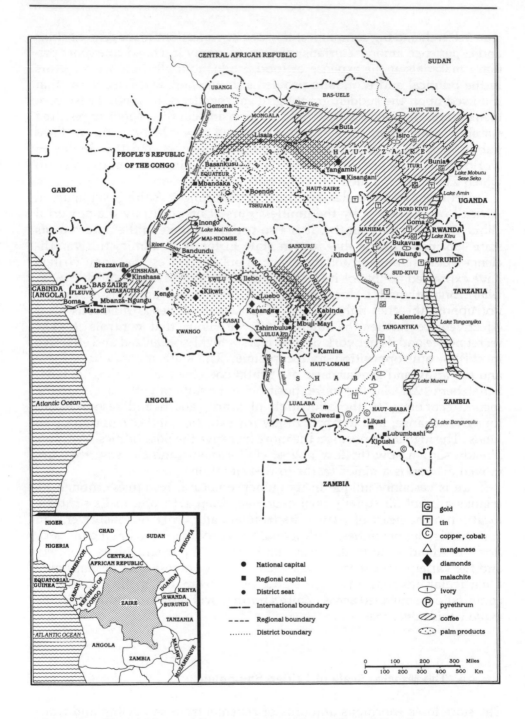

Map 1.1 *Zaire: Natural Resources and Agricultural Production*
(compiled by Janet MacGaffey)

has been smuggled or fraudulently exported: from 1975 to 1979 this illegal coffee trade was estimated to have cost Zaire $350 million (*Quarterly Economic Review, Ruanda and Burundi*, 1980). In 1979, the diamonds smuggled equalled in carats 68% of official exports, (5.5 million carats were smuggled; official production was 8.06 million) a loss of nearly $59 million (Bézy et al 1981:172). Massive quantities of cobalt, a primary mineral export, are smuggled and its revenues lost to the state; in 1985 the amount was estimated at 8,969 kg. (*Zaire Afrique*, 1985:635). By 1976 90% of ivory was smuggled (Kisangani 1985); exports were banned in 1978 but Zaire's vast elephant herds have all but disappeared under the continuing onslaught of poachers who sell to smugglers.[5]

Map 1.2 shows the principal food and export crops and minerals involved in smuggling, fraudulent export and barter across the borders that we detail in later chapters.

Our research investigated the effect of the 1983 fiscal and liberalization reforms which attempted to stop this drain of foreign exchange revenue. The artisanal production of diamonds and gold was legalized and licensed counters were set up for their purchase. This measure was apparently successful in decreasing diamond smuggling, since official diamond exports rose dramatically, tripling from 1983 to 1987. Gold exports likewise rose initially, but soon decreased again: they jumped from 2,100 kg. in 1982 to 5,200 kg. in 1983, but by 1986 they were down to 1,951 kg. (*Conjoncture Economique*, 1987:64).[6] Data from Kivu and Lower Zaire indicate that more gold is smuggled than is exported officially.

The reforms included liberalization of producer prices, but our studies in Kivu, Lower Zaire and Shaba show that this reform has not been put into effect in rural areas distant from the central government: price controls continue to be imposed with the result that food crops are extensively smuggled across the borders to take advantage of higher prices and acquire commodities scarce or unobtainable in Zaire.

These flows of unrecorded transborder trade (popularized as UTT for short, *Southern African Economist*, Dec. 88/Jan. 89) are defined as smuggling because they illegally cross national borders and evade tariffs, customs dues or regulations, but they are more appropriately seen as part of trade circuits within natural geographical regions. Some of these circuits are ancient.

Regional Trade Patterns and Their Historical Antecedents

Second economies are not a new phenomenon in Africa. Although little is written about them in historical accounts, we do get occasional glimpses. For example,

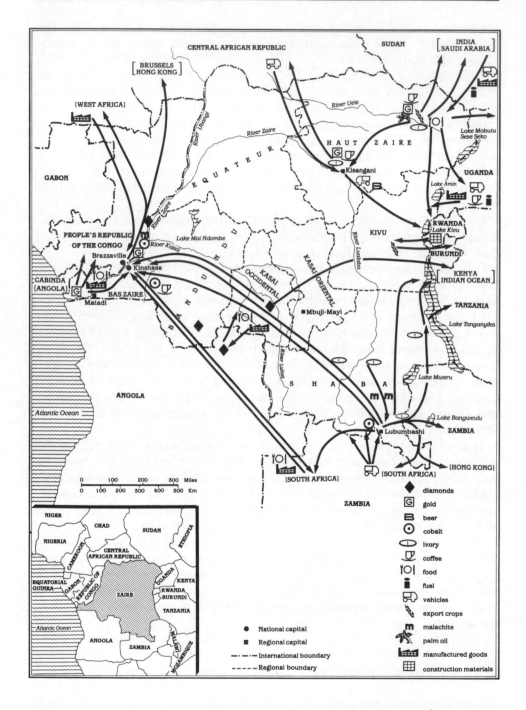

Map 1.2 *Principal Commodities Smuggled Across Zaire's Borders, 1987*
(compiled by Janet MacGaffey)

When the Portuguese took Sofala from the Muslims in 1506 it was intended that a royal monopoly should be imposed upon the trade. This proved unworkable, and instead an unofficial private trade developed, which was then taxed by the royal captains at Mozambique island. To avoid this taxation an illegal private trade grew up which was difficult to detect (Beach 1983: 259).

Ancient trade routes throughout Africa were originally established between natural regions offering different resources. They linked Africa's different peoples in trade networks extending over vast distances. Colonial powers imposed national boundaries, tariffs, trade restrictions and price controls, but people resisted colonial authority and continued to trade with each other. Traders revived ancient routes for smuggling and organized their own marketplaces for barter, bypassing official distribution systems.

This process of arbitrarily imposing borders divided peoples who formerly freely interacted, so that they found themselves on different sides of a frontier. Trade with each other, and the organization of trade further afield through co-operative networks were suddenly defined as illegal. This political development did not, however, necessarily prevent this trade: people continued old trading patterns, following old routes, but operating outside the official national economies to which they had been assigned. In the colonial period, people commonly fled across borders to escape taxes or local political upheavals. Devious routes for crossing frontiers came into being and facilitated the development of unrecorded transborder trade. Very little is known about the history of these more recent trading patterns; they constitute a fruitful topic for future research.

A recent publication of the World Bank identifies progress toward regional market integration as central to long-term development strategy in Africa. It points out the failure of co-operation through formal regional organizations: official figures show that intra-African trade is only at the level it was in the early seventies. Trade within ECOWAS, for example, comprises only about 3% of the group's international trade. The report, however, also emphasizes the sizeable volume of 'informal trade' across borders. It notes that this trade overcomes the constraints of poor transport and communications, generally cited as critical factors in the stagnation of intra-African trade (World Bank 1989: 149–162).

The massive extent of this unrecorded transborder trade in all regions of the African continent is evidence of market integration that people have brought about for themselves, outside official systems which have failed to carry out the necessary tariff reduction and other measures to promote such regional integration. Up to 70 administrative steps may be involved in moving commodities legally across African borders; in Zaire, for example, exports require 39 steps and imports 30 (World Bank 1989: 160–161). Such formalities strangle trade, so people have taken matters into their own hands. Should we look at smuggling as a spontaneous, popular

21

contribution to a kind of economic development that is in process, despite statistics to the contrary?

Since these flows of trade defy political boundaries, it is more realistic in assessing the economic situation in Africa to identify the trade circuits of geographical regions as well as focusing on national economies. The scale of this unofficial, unrecorded commerce is a measure of a much greater vigor of economic activity than is reflected in national accounts. 'Cross-border transactions are not a new phenomenon . . . What is new about this trade is its dramatic increase, both in volume and in its growth beyond the traditional exchange of goods' (Maliyamkono and Bagachwa 1990: 74). The regional trading circuits of this commerce are, in many cases, the means by which seemingly disastrous national economies manage to keep going.

This view of African economies demands a new approach, involving regional studies of these natural trade patterns. Igue Ogunsola has carried out such a study for West Africa in the sixties and seventies. He documents the dynamism of illegal trading sectors, for example, cocoa and palm products, imported manufactured goods and fuel smuggled between Benin and Nigeria; Ghanaian cocoa and diamonds smuggled to Togo in return for manufactured goods, building materials, alcohol, tobacco, cars and appliances; and peanuts smuggled extensively from Senegal to Gambia in exchange for imported consumer products (Igue 1976, 1977, 1983, 1985).

A more recent study by Kengne Fodouop (1988) details smuggling between Cameroon and Nigeria which has expanded since the Biafran war. According to one estimate, in 1985 Cameroon lost 68 billion CFA francs because of smuggling. Cameroon levies heavy taxes on imported goods to acquire hard currency and to protect its industry, which makes smuggling profitable, as does the periodic scarcity of goods. Border controls are lax. Commodities illegally traded include a wide range of foodstuffs and manufactured goods. Foods include dried fish, manioc, kola, livestock, fruit and vegetables. In 1984, 27,300 cattle for this illegal trade crossed at one entry post into Nigeria; in 1985, 1,150 tonnes of rice by this same post and to the north 1,206 tonnes of dried beans; and in 1986, through both posts, a total of 3,175 tonnes of dried fish. Manufactured goods traded in return are imported from all over the world; in 1986 they totalled 721,000 tonnes. Goods are moved along roads, along forest paths (by headload and pack saddle), or by waterways. This trade keeps markets well stocked in both countries, stimulates production, enables those who engage in it to earn a comfortable living, and keeps consumer prices down. In Cameroon, commodities smuggled from Nigeria are cheaper than those officially imported or locally produced.

An important factor in the success of this trade is that numerous Igbo people live on both sides of the border and have been active in organizing this commerce. Another factor is the strength of the CFA franc compared with the Nigerian naira, which has resulted in the development of a lively parallel money market on the frontier. Some 30,000 people are esti- mated to be involved in this illicit transborder trade, most of them young men with a low level of education. A majority of them trade about once a month to supplement another occupation, earning several thousand francs a year. It must be remembered, however, that the trade is difficult and risky.

This book documents regional trade in Central Africa in the eighties. Our three studies of unrecorded trade across Zaire's southern, northeastern and western borders show how the circulation of smuggled commodities links these three regions more closely to other countries than to the rest of Zaire (see Map 1.2). Northeastern Zaire is part of a regional area extending eastwards to the ports of the Indian Ocean and north to the Sudan, but only as far west as Kisangani. Shaba is tied to Zambia and South Africa and its trade in smuggled imports penetrates to Kasai and Kivu. Lower Zaire forms a regional trading area with the Democratic Republic of the Congo and Angola, including Cabinda. Beyond all these regions, trading ties for some commodities extend much further afield: to Europe, South and West Africa, India, and the Far East.

We will turn now to some of the policy implications of this discussion.

Policy Implications

In order to understand the real problems and constraints and the real potential and development possibilities of the Zairian economy, it is essential to take into account all the economic activity that is taking place. One of the most significant consequences of the vast size of the second economy is that Zaire's GDP is much larger and the economy more dynamic than it appears to be from the official figures. This has important implications for international aid donors, for potential investors, both foreign and national, and for government planners: clearly, they are underestimating the country's long-term investment needs, as well as its capacity to make use of increased investment. A better accounting framework, such as the one outlined earlier, must be a pressing priority.

Zaire's flourishing unrecorded trade of luxury consumer goods documented in later chapters, such as electrical appliances, expensive imported wax-print cloth, jewelry, shoes and handbags, indicates that, despite the general hardships in daily living, there is still a sizeable solvent demand, providing considerable market opportunities. If unrecorded trade across borders is taken into account, it is clear that intra-African trade between Zaire and its sub-Saharan neighbors is much great than official inter-regional trade figures indicate. Inter-regional co-operation is thus already

23

operating at an unofficial level. Within the continent as a whole, some kind of multi-country management of economies needs to build on what is already happening, by legitimizing it. Past experience with economic unions does not leave much room for optimism: they always seem to fall apart. Success might be more likely if management focused on specifics, such as relaxing tariffs on certain kinds of goods, removal of overly complex regulations, building up the infrastructure, and so on (The World Bank already puts priority on building up the transportation infrastructure, one of Zaire's most desperate needs).

Governments must confront the reality for people at all levels of society, which is that they need to increase their incomes above their salaries many times over. Obviously only some of this additional money can come from salary raises. Policy makers need to facilitate ways and means for extra income that are least harmful to the functioning of the economy and society. For example, government officials might resort less to bribery and corruption if restrictive regulations on their participation in business were removed, and if they were allowed to remain in one place long enough for entering business to be practicable.

Legal reform is the most critical of all, as De Soto has made abundantly clear. 'Legal institutions, rather than constituting an instrument for the development of Third World countries, are the principal obstacle to it' (De Soto 1989: xxii). In Peru, he finds that informal enterprises suffer not only from the costs of being illegal, but also because good laws to guarantee and promote their economic efficiency are lacking. Our studies show the difficulty of implementing the liberalization reforms in Zaire. 'Structural adjustment is not the same as institutional reform . . . without the institutional reforms to go with the policy changes, those countries that implement these programs will adopt the trappings of free markets but will continue to lack the legal institutions that ensure the political and social viability of economically sound policies' (ibid: xxvii).

Notes

1. They have been excellently summarized by Mkandawire (1986).
2. I am much indebted to Mr Cour for permission to use these ideas and for the important contribution they make to this study.
3. In Lubumbashi in 1986, a 50 kg. sack of Zambian maize flour retailed for 460 Z, a Zairian for 670 Z (Flouriot 1986: 17).
4. Zaire's colonial and post-colonial experiences have been richly detailed, see Young 1965; Callaghy 1984; Schatzberg 1988; Young and Turner 1985.
5. From information available at time of going to press, the October 1989 world ban on ivory trading agreed to by 90 countries, that came into effect in January 1990, appears to have decreased the demand for ivory and forced prices down by 50% (*Wall Street Journal* Feb., 1990). Poaching has reportedly declined in Kenya and Tanzania since the ban; in China and Hong Kong, ivory-carving factories have virtually closed down. Conservationists are encouraged by the poor prices African poachers are getting for ivory: at Kismayu, a transit point for ivory on the southern coast of

Somalia, it was being sold with difficulty in the early summer of 1990 for only $2 to $3 a kilogram (*New York Times*, May 22, 1990). A year previously it fetched $50 to $70 a kilogram (*Newsweek* April 16, 1990).

6. Gold and diamond counter fees were $60,000 for an initial guarantee, $5,000 for annual fees and an *ad valorem* tax on exports of 1.5%. In 1983, guarantees amounted to $3,410,000, annual fees to $1,550,000 and *ad valorem* to $1,858,640 (Tshibanza and Tshimanga, 1985: 339).

2

Historical, Cultural and Structural Dimensions of Zaire's Unrecorded Trade
JANET MACGAFFEY

The first chapter focused primarily on political economy. The second will provide some historical context and background information and take a more anthropological viewpoint, commenting on the social organization, social relations and cultural patterns of unrecorded trade. It is in these socio-cultural features, as succeeding chapters show, that the macro-level structures of political economy are manifested through the activities and strategies of individuals. After a brief historical outline and some detail on the economic crisis, we will describe the growth of the alternative distribution system, and then look at the personal ties on which unrecorded trade relies for its organization. They are of two kinds: bilateral ties based on clientship, and multilateral ties based on the networks and groups to which people belong, such as family, kinship and ethnicity. We will then consider some of the gender issues that emerge as integral elements in the functioning of the second economy. The chapter will end by drawing together the material from these sections and tying them into the first chapter, in an exploration of the political implications of the second economy and its significance for the process of class formation.

Historical and Economic Background[1]

Zaire is one of Africa's wealthiest countries in terms of natural resources. Its primary exports are copper, cobalt, diamonds, crude oil, and coffee. It has, nevertheless, a per capita income that is among the lowest in the world and official figures show a spiralling decline in the economy since the mid-seventies. This longstanding problem has complex roots: Belgian colonial policy, the turbulent events following independence in 1960, the disastrous indigenization of the economy, the decline in world market prices for the primary commodities that are the country's primary exports, and the nature of the new dominant class.

In 1908, following international outcry over the atrocities of King

26

Leopold's Congo Free State, Belgium established its colony of the Belgian Congo, which lasted until independence in 1960. Belgian colonialism was unparalleled in the continent in its control and penetration of African society, organized by the 'trinity' of bureaucracy, capital and the church (Young 1965: 32). Belgian administration was much denser than that of other colonial powers in Africa, and Africans could not rise above the level of clerk in the colonial bureaucracy.

The Catholic church received the full support of the colonial administration and ran most of the schools. Land grants to the missions could be used for commercial purposes as well as for self-support; as a result, the church became both wealthy and powerful. It remains one of the most effective organizations in the country, and one of the few powerful enough openly to criticize the government. Until 1954, almost all education was in the hands of the missions. Although the colony had one of the highest literacy rates in Africa, secondary education was minimal, and Africans could not rise above the level of clerk in the bureaucracy. At independence there were only a handful of university graduates and a few hundred with post-secondary professional training.

The colonial government granted huge concessions to the big mining and plantation companies, as well as an unusual degree of support for obtaining land and labor. The multinational companies entrenched in this period still dominate Zaire's economy. The Belgians frustrated the development of indigenous enterprise by denying Africans access to the more profitable sectors of the economy and to credit.

The colonial African elite thus lacked education, administrative and managerial experience, and wealth. At independence the Belgians handed over political but not economic control, so that the new dominant class based its power on control of the state, while ownership of the economy remained in the hands of the big foreign mining and plantation companies. The new Democratic Republic of the Congo was a typical peripheral capitalist economy, dependent on the export of primary products and ruled by a comprador bourgeoisie.

The Belgians had ill prepared the country for independence and political and economic chaos followed. The army mutinied; Katanga, the richest copper mining province, seceded; Belgian personnel fled; and the country was swept by rebellions. These events and the patrimonial politics of the First Republic for the next five years resulted in rapid decentralization of the state. This period ended with the rebellions of 1964–65 and the coup in which Mobutu Sese Seko took over as head of state in 1965. He recentralized the government and founded the single party of the MPR in 1967.

Under the Mobutu regime, the state increased participation in the productive sector, taking over Union Minière, the giant Belgian copper mining company in 1966–67, and turning it into the 100% state-owned corporation GECAMINES. 1968–1974 was a period of economic growth

from high copper prices. But in the early seventies, unwise public investments in prestigious luxury or military expenditures left a legacy of a
burgeoning national debt after copper prices dropped in 1974. . A new
co-operative relationship arose between the state and foreign interests: the
state took over ownership of large foreign enterprises, allocating management to a consortium or multinational; in 1969, the new Code of Investments liberalized the conditions for foreign investment. The centralization
of political power under Mobutu was accompanied by a concentration of
economic revenues in the hands of a small circle owing personal allegiance
to the president.

In the mid-seventies, an economically disastrous process of indigenization sent Zaire into a spiralling economic crisis. In 1973, the decrees of
Zairianization handed over foreign-owned businesses to Zairians, either to
the state or to individuals. New owners were all too often government
personnel or their friends and relatives. Some obtained vast holdings; few
had any serious entrepreneurial intentions or skills. By 1974 commerce
and agriculture were seriously disrupted and state revenues had sharply
declined. Concomitantly, world petroleum prices tripled, copper prices
dropped, the prices of industrial imports rose, and mineral exports were
disrupted by the closing of the Benguela railroad because of the Angolan civil war. The economy plunged into a crisis from which it has not
recovered. In 1975, the state attempted to control the situation with the
decree of Radicalization, by which it took over all large-scale enterprise.
But politics rather than competence governed the selection of the directors
of these enterprises, and by 1976 the government issued the decree of
Retrocession, returning businesses to their former foreign owners with
mandatory Zairian partners. In 1977 and 1978, the economic crisis dee-
pened after the invasions of Shaba and the disruption of the copper mining.

By 1978, output was 17% below the level of 1974, and imports 50%
below. The manufacturing sector was operating at only 40% of capacity; inflation was almost 100%; and real wages and salaries were one
quarter of their 1970 level. By 1979, industry was operating at one quarter
to one half capacity. A year later, the foreign debt had reached $5 billion.
Concomitantly, the administrative capacity of the state had drastically
declined.

Various attempts to address these problems included the 1979–1981
Mobutu Plan for economic development, foreign assistance programs, and
the use of expatriates to try and improve bureaucratic functioning. But
these efforts were all sabotaged by the elite's relentless pursuit of its own
interests. Zaire continually defaulted on its debts in the years that followed but always somehow negotiated rescheduling payment. In 1983,
a new agreement with the IMF for debt rescheduling included a 77.5%
devaluation of the zaire to cut down the parallel money market, and the
liberalization reforms. Zaire co-operated in a comprehensive IMF austerity
program, but the expected increased investment from donors did not

materialize. By 1987, the reform process had again broken down, the zaire depreciated further and inflation rose to over 50%.

This outline of events is summarized chronologically in Table 2.1.

Table 2.1 Chronology

1908	Belgian Congo founded
1960	Independence
1964–65	Rebellions
1965	Mobutu Sese Seko President
1967	Founding of MPR
1968–74	High copper prices and economic growth
1969	Code of Investments
1973	Decree of Zairianization
1975	Decree of Radicalization
1976	Decree of Retrocession
1977–78	Shaba Wars
1979–81	Mobutu Plan
1983	Liberalization Reforms

The Expansion of Unrecorded Trade

Unrecorded trade has expanded as the marketing structures of the official economy have deteriorated to the point where they barely function. Roads have deteriorated catastrophically since independence for lack of maintenance. In some regions, the official marketing system became almost defunct after Zairianization, when the big foreign companies organizing marketing were indigenized and many closed down. Other regions suffer from shortages of fuel, vehicles and spare parts, resulting from the chronic shortage of foreign exchange. For petty producers, prices are derisory in terms of purchasing power, and the goods they want to buy are scarce as well as high-priced in the few stores to be found in rural areas; marketing information and essential inputs are lacking, and credit is virtually unobtainable. For farmers and petty traders, the government is capricious and oppressive: local administration is out of reach of the central government whose decrees it does not always implement, and is drastically short of financial and other resources. Few local government personnel have adequate training and experience and all are grossly under-paid; they extract what they can from the local population in a pattern of payoffs, corruption and extortion. For all these reasons, the official economy is unpredictable and irrational in its mode of operation.

Yet in this situation of extreme difficulty, urban growth presents the opportunity of a greatly expanding food market. Bjorn Beckman comments that in Nigeria the official assessment of the stagnation and decline of agriculture conceals a major and dynamic change in the development of Nigerian capitalism: the dramatic expansion of commercial agriculture to supply the domestic food market (Beckman 1987: 110; 115–117). Decline in export production in Nigeria is largely attributable to a major shift into production for this domestic market. He refers to this phenomenon as 'the new food frontier', and stresses that the backbone of such expansion has been peasant small-holder production. It is small peasant farmers who provide the bulk of the food for the non-agricultural population (Beckman 1988: 36). Zaire's cities, like Nigeria's have shown rapid growth since independence, but the deficiencies of local government administration and the inadequacy of the marketing and transportation infrastructure create enormous difficulties for rural producers on Zaire's 'food frontier'. The various forms of unrecorded trade of the second economy have arisen as people attempt to surmount these difficulties and take advantage of the new opportunities.

The organization of this trade depends to a great extent on personal ties. The trust and confidence inspired by personal relationships or common cultural background provide the reliability and predictability that are so conspicuously lacking in the official system. As Maliyamkono and Bagachwa point out (1990: 119–120), such organization is not politically threatening and does not rely on political and economic power centers. We will now examine various kinds of personal ties: first patron-client ties, then those based on family, kinship and ethnicity. We will see that each primarily benefits different categories of people.

The Organization of the Second Economy: the Importance of Personal Ties[2]

Clientship
Eric Wolf comments that ties of clientship are

> especially functional in situations where the formal institutional structure of society is weak and unable to deliver a sufficiently steady supply of goods and services, especially to the terminal levels of the social order (Wolf 1966: 17).

In Zaire, traders, petty producers, truckers and retailers have set up an unofficial system of distribution and marketing, sometimes over enormous distances, that, in large measure, provides the food supply for cities and towns and supplies the rural areas with the goods agricultural producers want to buy. Much of this trade is illegal because it avoids taxation and licensing fees, involves smuggling and barter, or in other ways evades state control. Patron-client ties are one of the means by which this system operates.

Makwala gives details in chapter 4 of patron-client ties set up between trader and farmer through pre-harvest cash advances, between truckers and client traders who travel their routes regularly and are given reduced freight rates, and between traders and the market retailers they finance through short-term credit when they sell the food crops they bring from rural areas for Kinshasa's markets. Rukarangira and Schoepf also report clientship networks between traders and producers in the maize trade in North Shaba. Other studies show that the rice trade of Upper Zaire likewise operates through client relations. From the late seventies, when rice mills were moved from the interior to the city because of the fuel crisis and the deterioration of rural roads, unlicensed traders have proliferated in the rice trade around Kisangani. They go into areas not covered by the 'official' rice traders to buy crops that would otherwise rot for lack of buyers. They buy, at prices higher than the 'official' price, paddy and rice which has been manually and illegally husked by farmers. Both men and women are included among these traders; sixteen of the twenty surveyed had regular clients among the producers from whom they bought rice (Russell 1989: 7–8, 11).

This state of affairs has developed in the last fifteen years. It represents a change in the previously existing pattern of political patron-clientage, of dyadic ties between the politically powerful and their supporters. These new client relations have developed in a different sector of the population, among small producers, traders, truckers and retailers. They provide more reliable and predictable trading relations than does the official system, but, as Makwala shows, they benefit traders at the expense of small farmers.

These farmers lack marketing options: for many the only opportunity to sell their crops comes from entering into client relations with one of the unlicensed traders who travel through the rural areas buying up produce. The terms of this clientage favor the traders because, although interest is not overtly paid on cash advances, the low prices paid for farm produce, compared to prices of goods the producers need to buy, represent implicit interest rates and are a form of usurious extraction.[3] The cash advances of the traders are essential to the producer for his farming, to buy tools, seeds and other inputs, and to maintain his family. They tie him to a particular trader and the price he or she offers, which is set at a rate so low that all risk is transferred to the borrower and price fluctuations operate to the advantage of the lender. This situation has been described as 'forced commerce'.[4] Securities such as standing crops are grossly undervalued in relation to what the lender expects to be their market value. This under-valuing results partly from the monopoly power of the lender and partly from the personalized nature of the relationship in which the loan is made (Bhaduri 1983: 76).

Beckman finds that moneylending between patrons and clients likewise pervades the peasant economy in Nigeria. It follows patron-client net-works as peasants at all levels borrow money to pay for production needs, social obligations and emergencies. Borrowing by the better off is linked to investment, such as buying land and inputs and hiring labor. 'Moneylending is exploitative' he says, 'but in the foreseeable future there are no political forces capable of providing an alternative to those exploi-tative relations and the crude "social security" provided by patron-client relations' (Beckman 1988: 39).

Other personal ties operate, however, that are not basically extractive but instead can be seen as social assets for the poor.

Family, Kinship and Ethnicity
The regional studies that follow provide many examples of the use of family bonds, kinship relations and ethnic connections for gaining access to goods or other resources for second economy activities, for practical help in facilitating these activities or reducing their costs, and for support-ing mutual trust and co-operation. In order to acquire scarce goods from wholesalers, or to import goods illegally, it is very important to have a connection with someone working in one of the wholesale houses to facili-tate access to scarce goods, and a partner living in the country from which goods are imported who can acquire and ship them. Entrance to certain smuggling networks depends on membership of a particular ethnic group and knowledge of its language. Where transport costs are inordinately high and space scarce, those with personal ties with riverboat captains, airline personnel and truckers have the advantage of reducing costs and ensuring space for their freight. When credit is unobtainable from the banks and borrowing at usurious rates is the alternative, interest-free loans from kinsmen or the mutual rotating credit associations of *likelemba* or *musiki*, small groups with close ties between members, depend on the trust that comes from personal relationships. The common cultural background and loyalties of those from the same ethnic group, and the mutual obliga-tions and emotional bonds of family and kinship, all operate to promote the trust, accountability and sense of moral responsibility that is lack-ing in the official economy and that contributes to its irrationality and unpredictability.

Vijay Jagannathan describes personal ties as social assets that create earning opportunities for the poor. When behavioral relations have a pro-ductive element because they are used to create wealth through a steady

32

generation of income over time, they can be described as social assets (Jagannathan 1987: 29, 108).

> Simple multilateral relations generate informal property rights in the organized sectors of the economy by restricting access to them. As these rights are quickly converted to tangible property, they are virtually indistinguishable from tangible property rights (ibid: 81).

These relations of clan, caste or tribe can be used to capture rent-seeking opportunities. Poor people use the informal contracts these relations create as endogenous social security nets (ibid: 66, 129). In Zaire, such relations are used not only to create rent-seeking opportunities but to organize reliably the most ordinary economic transactions.

Such ties among those who are operating outside the formal economy can be seen as the counterpart among the poor to the rent-seeking opportunities of those who work in public institutions. As President Mobutu himself has put it:

> Everything is for sale, everything is bought in our country. And in this traffic, holding any slice of public power constitutes a veritable exchange instrument, convertible into illicit acquisition of money or other goods, or the evasion of all sorts of obligations (quoted in Callaghy 1984: 190).

Here, as Jagannathan points out, officials take advantage of their position to enter into corrupt agreements and can thus acquire earning capabilities to which they are not legally entitled. Such rent-seeking opportunities come from the relative scarcity of administrative agencies, which means that citizens have to beat the system by social connections or through bribes to acquire what are ostensibly free public services. These opportunities constitute a market response to scarcity (Jagannathan 1987: 109–114). Any kind of employment, as Alain Morice points out, in circumstances similar to Zaire in Guinea and Angola, represents social capital: it brings the possibility of rendering services, creating obligations and receiving other services in return. Participation in such trafficking is a vital necessity for everyone in order to survive (Morice 1985: 112; 1987: 115). Zairians who do not have jobs, survive to a great extent through the social assets they gain from ties of family, kinship and ethnicity.

Family and kinship ties also represent assets because they form the basis for the delayed reciprocity of a non-monetized exchange between urban and rural areas. Foodstuffs produced by farmers are sent to kin in the towns, for them to live on or to sell, and manufactured goods and other commodities scarce and expensive in the rural areas, are sent in return by urban relatives. This form of exchange, extremely widespread, is an important mechanism for dealing with the problem of high prices and scarcity. Makwala's and Walu and Schoepf's chapters show details of its operation. Appadurai has shown the falsity of a sharp distinction between barter and gift exchange and commodity exchange. A calculative dimension exists in all of them, though they vary in the associated form and intensity of sociality (Appadurai 1986: 13). 'Barter, as a form of trade . . . links the exchange of commodities in widely different social, technological and institutional circumstances. Barter may thus be regarded as a special form of commodity exchange, one in which, for any variety of reasons, money plays either no role or a very indirect role (as a mere unit of account)' (ibid: 10). Vwakyanakazi's chapter documents the existence of markets for the smuggling trade operating entirely by barter. The rural urban exchange between kin is a variant in this special form of commodity exchange. Appadurai emphasizes the absence of social, political and cultural norms in exchange by barter (ibid: 11). The exchange between rural and urban kin in Zaire, however, is an interesting variant. It operates as a form of delayed barter, regulated and motivated by the social and cultural norms of kinship.

As well as constituting social assets in the form of earning-opportunities or sources of food and consumer goods, family and kinship ties also have a levelling function. Obligations attaching to family and kinship relations result in some redistribution of wealth. Town-dwellers can be called upon to house relatives, temporarily or permanently, while they search for work, attend school or just need living space. All the households in Walu and Schoepf's study in chapter 5 include such relatives. Townsfolk feel under a heavy obligation to pay for the schooling and/or support of poorer kin, a considerable burden for them. In some instances, though by no means always, those in town receive household help, childcare or unpaid labor in business enterprise in return for the assistance they give.

Gender and the Second Economy

Gender is an important dimension of any examination of the second economy; the ongoing struggle to adjust the relative position of men and women is very evident in some of its activities.

Zaire is a male-dominated society and its formal institutional structure constrains women's economic activities. A woman must have her husband's permission to take out a trading license or to open a bank account. If her husband has contributed goods or capital to her commerce, she does not have the sole right to her earnings. If her husband objects to her taking a job, a letter from him can nullify her employment contract. A woman can escape the restrictions imposed by the official institutional structure to some degree, however, by operating in the second economy: here she needs no license or bank account and has no employment contract.[5]

In rural society, women traditionally provided the food for their families and had their own budgets, separate from their husband's. Once the family was fed, a woman's surplus product was her own. During the colonial period, the position of women in society was marginalized. Opportunities for education, necessary for any effective participation in the new economy, were minimal for women and, anyway, married women were often discouraged from working by their husbands. Colonial restrictions discriminated against women in the movement to the towns; the only means for them to make money was by selling domestic services, including sex. Since independence, the situation has changed: the decline in real wages has made it imperative that women contribute to household expenses. Given their lack of skills and the discrimination which, though against the law, they face in the formal job market, they have found that their best opportunities lie in second economy trade. They have taken it up everywhere in Zaire's towns and cities. The result of this change is that women have once again become the major food providers for households.

A series of studies of Kinshasa in 1969, 1975 and 1986, directed by Joseph Houyoux, give us a remarkable time depth in which to follow the process of this change. They show how steeply the percentage of household income represented by salaries has declined, dramatically highlighting the expansion of the second economy and the changing role of women in the urban economy. In 1969, salaries made up 99.1% of the income of officials, 70% of the income of other wage earners (Houyoux 1973: 129); by 1975 they made up only 62% of the needs of officials, and 51% and 47% of other categories (Houyoux and Kinavwuidi 1986: 173); by 1986 only 33% of the income of officials, 42% of the income of salaried workers, and 37–47% for the different categories of laborers came from wages and salaries (see above, Houyoux et al. 1986: 35). Houyoux assumed that a large percentage of unknown sources of household income came from family enterprise. Walu's data show that such enterprise primarily consists of women's trade, and that earnings from it generally pay for the food consumed by the household. This trade is largely unlicensed and evades tax.

Women's trade was already a primary source of essential additional household income in 1969, giving them a greater degree of autonomy and independence in city life than they had in the colonial period. Houyoux's studies show the importance of this trade for essential household support at this time and quotes comments of individual women on the independence they perceive they have gained from being able to earn money in this way. As early as 1969, some women had moved from petty trade into large-scale and profitable commerce, importing and exporting goods to the interior and overseas (Houyoux 1973: 244). By 1987 a number of women had become extremely wealthy in such activities. Schoepf and Walu document examples of such trade; they show that only women of high socioeconomic position have the contacts and capital necessary to carry on this more profitable commerce. Like all enterprise in the current socio-political situation it is highly precarious, but women are finding opportunities that did not exist for them before and some are achieving impressive success.[6]

Poor women, on the other hand, lead frantic and marginal existences, desperately trying to feed their children on small returns from petty commerce.

Married women continue to be particularly susceptible to the controls of the formal institutional structure, which is manipulated by men to serve their own interests. The new Family Code (Law 87-010, Article 496) states that the management of goods acquired by the wife in her profession shall be performed by her, unless this goes against the 'household's harmony and monetary interests' (*portent atteinte à l'harmonie et aux intérêts pécuniaires du ménage*), in which case the husband may take over their management. Clearly, the definition of this situation is wide open to interpretations favoring men. Demands by husbands in some of the trader's stories in chapter 5, for 'transparent' financial management of their wives' affairs, reflect this shift in the formal legal system that has taken place to counteract the perceived threat to men in the new economic power some women are achieving.

Making Ends Meet or Getting Rich: Class, Politics and the Second Economy

What are the political implications of so much activity outside state control but in which state-linked personnel often play a role? What sort of challenge does the second economy offer to the state? Most of the literature on 'informal economies' has emphasized their economic significance, but some writers have focused on their political aspect. Hernando de Soto calls it the 'invisible revolution' in the Third World. In particular, in Peru, he calls the informal economy, existing largely outside the law, a hidden revolution that is 'the Other Path', the peaceful, non-violent alternative to the violent revolutionary Shining Path guerrilla movement (De Soto 1989). In the socialist economy of Hungary, Ivan Szelenyi finds private producers among peasants and workers forming a new class of 'socialist entrepreneurs' which has forced concessions from bureaucrats in a 'silent revolution from below' (Szelenyi 1988: 4–5). In Africa, Maliyamkono and Bagachwa consider that although the 'informal sector' has always been regarded as non-threatening, 'in its new and excessive form, however, the over-expansion of the informal sector poses a challenge to the state legitimacy of many African countries' (Maliyamkono and Bagachwa 1990: 35).

In Zaire, the second economy has expanded enormously as the administrative capacity of the state has declined with the increase in rent-seeking activities of state personnel. An obvious question is why do people continue to work at jobs at all when salaries are so inadequate and better money can be made in independent enterprise on the margins of the law, or in some sort of hustle? For the majority, the primary importance of a job is not its miserable wages but the useful contacts it brings, the access it offers to resources, and its opportunities to allocate scarce commodities or to extort from those lower down the social scale, all of which are points of entry to the second economy.

What sort of challenge does the second economy offer to the state? As Schatzberg has pointed out, the state has become a fluid, shifting entity (Schatzberg 1988: 142). Officials are continually moving from one post to another: in any one locality this means constant changes in policy and in the degree of enforcement of regulations, constant shifts in the areas of corruption, and a continual state of uncertainty for the general population over the degree of oppression, or the windows of opportunity, that may occur. In the situation of general uncertainty and economic crisis, everyone has some sort of hustle, in order to survive and to attempt to find a way to improve their lives. But these activities do not offer an overt threat to the state: people say 'we are too busy fending for ourselves (*débrouillements personelles*)'. It is not only the secret police and the state monopoly of force that have stifled political opposition. Mobutu's encouragement of the second economy in his advice to the population to '*Débrouillez-vous*' is one measure of his political skill.

Nevertheless, a considerable shift in Zairian society has been brought on by this vast expansion of the second economy: the economic base of the class structure has changed. During the colonial period, the Belgians and the multinationals controlled the economy. At independence the new national government gained political but not economic control; the new dominant class, a classic comprador bourgeoisie, based its power on control of the state and alliance with the agents of multinational capitalism. After Mobutu came to power in 1965, the strategy for the reconstruction of the state was to develop a public sector strong enough to serve the economic interests of this new state-based class, but it failed when indigenization of foreign-owned enterprise resulted in economic chaos and as the administrative capacity of the state declined. This class is essentially parasitic on the economy; it does not control it but uses state position to serve personal interests and to restrict the economic opportunities of other classes. This is a major reason why the state has become increasingly ineffective in regulating the economy, evident in its widespread inability to implement regulations, taxation and border controls. The same phenomenon is observed in Tanzania:

> [the] growth of the second economy in Tanzania is seen as a reflection of the weakening of state control, and not only the inability of the state to provide the basic needs of the masses but also its ineffectiveness in controlling and co-ordinating its excessive interventionist programmes (Maliyamkono and Bagachwa 1990: 49).

37

I have shown elsewhere that a local capitalist class is in process of formation in Zaire, to which wealth accumulated in the second economy has been a contributing factor (MacGaffey 1987). It was beyond the scope of the present study to document this process further, but profits from smuggling and other second economy activities have been one source of capital for investment in substantial manufacturing, and in agro-business producing for the local market as well as for export, in commerce, and in real estate. The nascent bourgeoisie enjoys a middle-class lifestyle, educates its children through university, and passes on wealth to them; it is thus beginning to reproduce itself as a class.

The second shift is in the gradual but huge expansion in the number of second economy transport, construction, trading and manufacturing enterprises (see MacGaffey 1991). An informal transport system exists in Kinshasa that carries almost as many passengers as the parastatal bus company (Baehrel et al 1985); the informal construction sector of the city accounts for 70% of the growth in the residential area and houses two thirds of the population (Delis and Girard 1985); a survey by the ILO in the mid-eighties reported 12,000 manufacturing, retail and service enterprises in the city's informal sector. But this burgeoning of the second economy does not only take place in the capital. The chapters that follow detail the extent, nature and earnings of unrecorded trade, between rural and urban areas and across Zaire's borders, showing that these illegal activities bring in much higher earnings than are possible in the formal wage and salary sector.[7] Precarious and uncertain though it may be, making money by illicit means can bring higher returns than salaried employment and lawful business. If one venture fails, another may succeed. Our studies also show that small farmers, rural workers, village chiefs and hunters can better their lot through participation in the second economy. The state is incapable of clamping down on all this activity, and anyway the economy cannot function without it. Such enterprise has come to constitute an economic base for the subordinated classes that they did not enjoy in the early years of the regime. This change, precarious and tentative though it may be, represents a significant power shift in society. Its long-term political implications are still in question.

As stated above, one reason the state cannot clamp down on the second economy is that the wealthy and powerful consolidate their own position through participation in its activities. Certain state personnel and professionals use their office, influence or contacts to acquire commodities for smuggling, fraudulent export, barter, and speculation, or to engage in bribery, corruption and embezzlement. Some of them become enormously wealthy by these means. The extremely lucrative opportunities available to personnel at all levels of government, including customs officials, means that immense vested interests stand in the way of any reform of the system. It is not in the individual or class interests of government personnel to implement such measures. Great practical difficulties stand in the way of reforms anyway, because of the decline in the administrative capacity of the state; they often could not be implemented even if the officials involved wanted to carry them out, but mostly they do not want to. Our data show that although the policy framework is set up, it cannot be implemented because of political limitations and corruption. Not only are people dependent on the second economy to provide wealth, or even a decent livelihood, those in high social position often depend on being able to offer their supporters and clients opportunities to acquire goods or to dispense services lucratively. Reforms will only work when Zaire's political structure changes and they serve the interests of government officials at all levels.

In the second economy, people are taking matters into their own hands and organizing an unofficial system; they are compensating for the inability of the state to supply the infrastructure, services, and protection of individual rights the citizens of any nation need and expect. This process, in De Soto's words, shows that 'people are capable of violating a system which does not accept them, not so that they can live in anarchy but so that they can build a different system which respects a minimum of essential rights' (De Soto 1989: 55). We will see how successful they have been by turning now to the regional studies. Does the second economy have beneficial effects? To what extent does it compensate for the deficiencies of the official system? What are its disadvantages and harmful effects? Does it constitute a peaceful hidden revolution such as De Soto finds in Peru?

Notes

1. The principal sources for this section are Bézy 1981, Callaghy 1984, Leslie 1987, Schatzberg 1980, Young 1965, Young and Turner 1985.
2. The ideas discussed in this section of the chapter were included in papers presented at seminars at the Hoover Institution, Stanford University, April 1989, at the African Studies Centre, Cambridge University, May 1989, and at the meetings of the American Anthropological Association, November 1989, Washington DC. I am grateful to participants at all three for helpful comments and criticism.
3. Basu considers that the underpricing of collateral is an implicit interest rate, with the implication that the absence of high interest rates cannot be equated with the absence of usurious extraction (Basu 1984: 146).
4. 'It is particularly at such historical junctures, when the populist State in a predominantly agrarian economy is not relying heavily on its legal-administrative coercive power to extract a large 'tribute' from any section of the peasantry that the method of forced commerce has a tendency to emerge as an important method in the process of extraction of agricultural surplus from the small peasants' (Bhaduri 1983: 11).
5. This argument is given in greater detail in MacGaffey 1988.
6. A similar situation is reported to be developing in Tanzania: 'Although the majority of women in the city are relegated to low-income-generating projects, women in the higher income brackets are involved in some of the most lucrative projects private citizens can engage in. Many of them have left professional or semi-professional jobs as secondary or vocational school instructors, nurses, accountants and secretaries to become the main breadwinner in the family through their projects, while their husbands retain their formal jobs and the status and connections that goes along with

them. Not more than five years ago it was virtually unheard of for women to be managing such ambitious private enterprises' (Tripp 1988: 11).
7. Marc Pain reports that the standard of living of traders and artisans in Kinshasa is superior to that of wage workers (Pain 1984: 131). De Soto finds that in Peru informal traders earn, on average, 38% more than the legal wage (De Soto 1989: 62).

II REGIONAL STUDIES

3 Import and Export in the Second Economy in North Kivu
VWAKYANAKAZI MUKOHYA[1]

Second economies pervade the countries of Black Africa and among them Zaire's *système D* is notorious.[2] But the mechanisms and strategies of any country's second economy vary considerably with the geographical and social environment; it can only be fully understood through regional studies. This chapter deals with North Kivu, an area of Zaire renowned for the proliferation of second economy activities. It focuses in particular on unrecorded import and export.

The data for the study was collected during field research from February to April 1987, mostly in the towns of Goma, Butembo and Beni. Second economy activities in North Kivu make up long chains linking many persons of variable wealth and economic success. The producers, small intermediaries, importers and exporters who make up these chains come from different social levels; a primary research task was to select informants to represent each of them. Methods of research consisted primarily of intensive interviewing of the traders involved, of government officials (in the local administration, the customs service and the Office of Economic Affairs), of young gold diggers, and of individuals engaged in various kinds of smuggling. Data was also gathered through surveys and from documentary sources: surveys of local markets and shops produced information on prices in the rural agglomerations of Kanyabayonga, Kaina, Kirumba and Oicha, and the towns of Butembo and Beni, along the main road, shown in Map 3.1; searches of local administrative reports, generally ill-kept, revealed some scanty information on the local second economy, usually in the form of complaints in passing, or comments that it was 'energetically fought' by means of 'appropriate' weapons (left unspecified).

Research on second economy activities has not been easy; its constraints and limitations are evident in our results. Since these activities are clandestine, they need to be observed over a relatively long period of time and two months was hardly sufficient. Difficulties in getting around presented another problem. Private transportation systems exist in the region but they were disrupted during the research period by the closing of roads

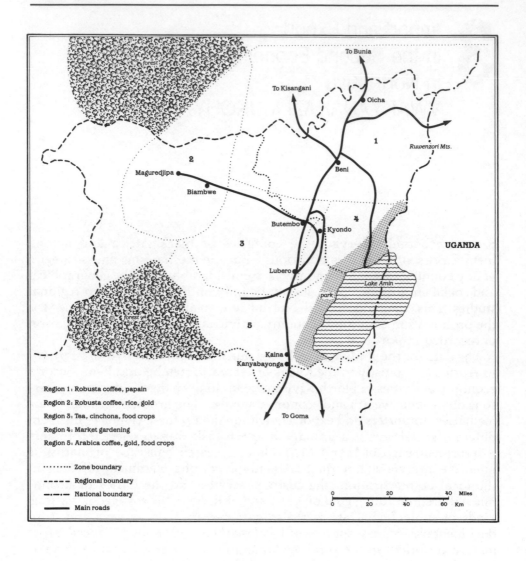

Region 1: Robusta coffee, papain
Region 2: Robusta coffee, rice, gold
Region 3: Tea, cinchona, food crops
Region 4: Market gardening
Region 5: Arabica coffee, gold, food crops

·········· Zone boundary
- - - - - Regional boundary
-·-·-·- National boundary
———— Main roads

Map 3.1 *Economic Regions of Beni and Lubero Zones of North Kivu*
(compiled by Vwakyanakazi Mukohya)

and the constant rise in fares. Furthermore, government offices distrust researchers and were uncomfortable answering questions about the second economy, especially since North Kivu is widely regarded as one of the primary regions for smuggling in Zaire. The data and figures available are thus fragmentary. There were advantages and disadvantages to being a native of the area. It certainly facilitated making contacts for the research and brought access to some documents that would have been refused to an investigator from elsewhere, since the social science researcher is easily taken for a state inspector or security agent in disguise. But being a local person was also costly in terms of time and financial resources.

Social and Economic Context

I selected the northern part of North Kivu for research, in particular the administrative zones of Lubero and Beni (see Map 3.2). It was impossible to extend fieldwork to the whole of North Kivu because of the short time allotted for the research, the ethnic diversity of the inhabitants, and the variation in geographical and socio-economic factors affecting living conditions in the region.

North Kivu is predominantly rural, with people subsisting mainly on agriculture and petty livestock raising. The southern part of the region consists of the administrative zones of Goma, Rutshuru, Masisi and Walikale. It is populated by Hutu, Hunde, Nyanga, and Nande immigrants, and is less densely populated than the north, especially on the eastern edges of the equatorial forest: Walikale has six inhabitants per square kilometer, Masisi 95 (*Gouvernorat du Kivu* 1985a: 4). The northern part consists of the zones of Beni and Lubero, populated primarily by Nande. The variation in altitude of Nande territory, from 1,600 to 2,300 metres, results in a number of microclimates and makes it possible to grow a range of crops, from coffee, tea, papain and pyrethrum, to wheat, market-gardening products, and food crops such as beans, cassava, bananas and sweet potatoes. Few people are in wage employment: those that are mostly work in local administration, education, banks and small agro-industrial enterprises.

Contributory factors to the expansion of the second economy in the area are proximity to the borders of Uganda, Rwanda, Kenya and the Sudan, and distance from any of Zaire's major cities: Kinshasa is 2,000 km., Kisangani 800 km., and Bukavu 500 km., over roads that are in very poor condition. Furthermore, Nande territory is bordered to the south and east by Virunga Park, one of Zaire's largest national parks. It covers about 8,000 sq.km., and is the largest after Upemba Park in Shaba (10,000 sq.km.) and bigger than Garumba Park in Upper Zaire

45

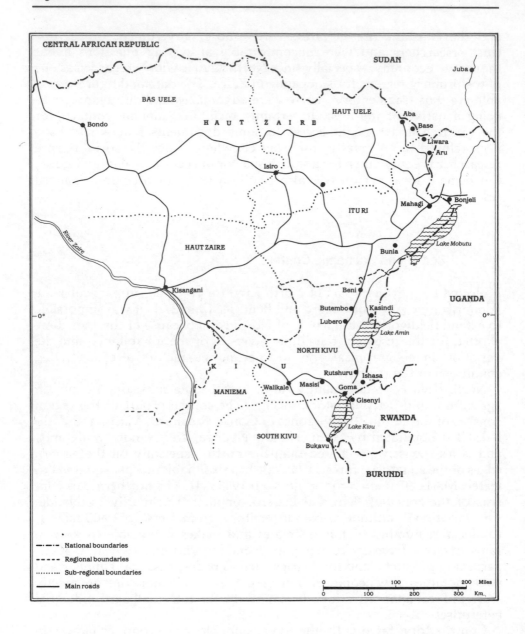

Map 3.2 *Geographic Region of Research (1987)*
(compiled by Vwakyanakazi Mukohya)

(5,000 sq.km.). Formerly the most diverse in terms of fauna and flora, it is being relentlessly stripped of its herds of elephants and other wild game by bands of young smugglers who are otherwise unemployed. The government's ability to control this situation continually deteriorates.

The Nande population of the zones of Beni and Lubero is expanding as follows:

1930	234,694
1960	467,504
1980	1,057,448
1985	11,166,941

Sources: (*Gouvernorat du Kivu* (1985); Kasay, (1983: 63–64)

In 1985 the average annual growth rate was estimated to be 3.56%.

Each zone serves as the hinterland of a rapidly growing urban center: Butembo, in the zone of Lubero, had a population of 100,000 in 1987, growing at an average annual rate of 10%, and Beni, in the zone of Beni, a population of 50,000, growing at a rate of 8% (*Gouvernorat du Kivu* 1985; Kasay, 1983: 127–129) The relative isolation of this area and the few opportunities for salaried employment for its expanding population[3] have given rise to some spectacular manifestations of the second economy, as people increasingly take up its activities for survival, self-protection and enrichment.

Commodities Traded in the Import/Export Sector of the Second Economy

It is difficult to come up with an exhaustive list of commodities making up the trade flows of the second economy. Firstly, because this economy is by definition underground, its operations and especially its revenues do not appear in official statistics. Secondly, North Kivu has many frontier posts. The official ones manned by ONEIDA (office of customs control) are Goma/Gisenyi, Rutshuru/Ishasa, and Beni/Kasindi (see Map 3.2). Unofficial ones are changeable and have no border control. Lake Kivu lies between North Kivu and Rwanda; Lake Amin between North Kivu and Uganda. The populations on both sides of the frontier, however, are linguistically and culturally related.

Dishonest customs agents at the official border crossings often actively participate in clandestine trade themselves and falsify their reports. They do not readily admit to these activities to the researcher for fear of the authorities and of losing their jobs and with them the very substantial extra income they can acquire. One minor customs official, for example, revealed that his superior brought home each day at least

10,000 Z; the share of the junior official was 5–600 Z for a 'bottle of beer'.

A list of the commodities exported and imported in the second economy can only be approximate. The ones most frequently traded are shown in Map 3.3.

Exports

The most important of the wide range of commodities produced in the region and exported in unrecorded trade are gold, ivory, and export crops, such as coffee, papain, tea and cinchona. Despite various constraints to be described later, Beni and Lubero zones are fertile areas for production of export crops, as shown in Table 3.4. According to local entrepreneurs all these products are smuggled, although it is difficult to estimate the quantity to any exact extent.

Table 3.4   Commercial Agricultural Production in Beni and Lubero Zones, End of 1985

Beni Zone	Area (in hectares)	Planters	Reported	Unreported	Total Production
Coffee: Arabica	19,927.43	39,500	19,438.30	489.13	9,719.190
Robusta	44,356.40	62,047	41,412.20	2,944.2	20,706.100
Cinchona	414	423	414	–	
Tea	457	CAK*	457	–	
Papaya	20,400.73	24,381	10,526.32	9,874.41	
Pyrethrum	5.20	5	5.20	–	
Lubero Zone					
Coffee: Arabica	1,498	2,974	1,372	126	686,000
Robusta	833	3,250	705	128	352,500
Cinchona	2,057	1,809	1,810	247	
Pyrethrum	416.99	10	416.99	–	

* Commission Agricole du Kivu

Coffee and Other Export Crops

It is possible to make a tentative estimate of the amount of coffee smuggled during the harvest months of January 1984–85 and 1985–86, through April.

In 1984–85 Lubero and Beni zones produced 31,463,790 kg. of coffee (Arabica and Robusta). They exported 21,973,940 kg., so a total of 9,489,850 kg. of the coffee produced does not appear in the official export figures. The quantity is too large to be accounted for by rejections by the local factory in the process of sorting and purifying before export, nor is it consumed locally, since the Nande do not drink coffee.

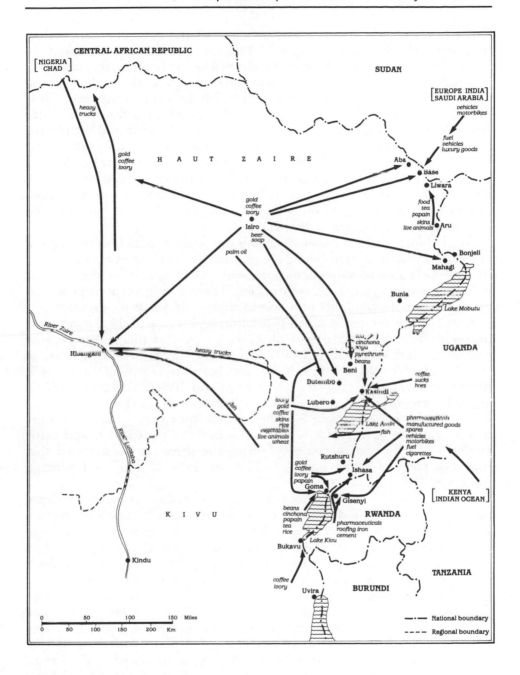

Map 3.3 *Principal Commodities of Unrecorded Trade in N.E. Zaire*
(compiled by Janet MacGaffey)

One can reasonably estimate that between 30 and 35% of local production was clandestinely exported. 1985–86 production increased to 129,000,000 kg., of which only 41,116,800 kg. was officially exported, according to OZACAF (the coffee marketing board), so that about 77,883,200 kg., or 60%, was exported through the second economy. These estimates do not, however, include the large quantities of coffee fraudulently imported into Beni and Lubero from Uganda and distributed through the second economy. During the coffee harvest, on average two Ugandan trucks full of coffee enter fraudulently each day at the border post of Ishasa/Rutshuru and about four at Kasindi/Beni.[4] This amounts to about 6,000 tonnes of coffee a year, 20–30% more than the 4–5,000 tonnes estimated to be smuggled out of the country north from Isiro in 1984 (*Conjoncture Economique* 1985: 41).

Local traders estimate that over half the local production of papain, tea and cinchona is fraudulently exported by local growers or buyers through Goma's international airport, with the co-operation of particular individuals among the local authorities. These commercial crops are all produced in both capitalist and non-capitalist modes of production.

A study of the present state of plantation agriculture in these zones does not exist: 'It is difficult to give an exact account of this sector because title is so often disputed' (CECOPANE, 1981–82, 3: 504). Beni zone at the end of 1978 had about 1600 ha. divided into 175 plantations: 64% Robusta coffee, 13% pasture, 2% papaya and 10% still abandoned.[5] In 1979, Lubero zone had a total area of 7,261 ha. divided into 96 plantations. The acreage of about 20 others is not known . . . Plantations are mostly given over to coffee (1,442 ha.), cinchona (1,305 ha.), and cattle raising (2,129 ha.), or a combination of the three. It is estimated that four big planters alone hold 1,943 ha. or 25% of the total acreage' (ibid: 504–508).

In spite of the domination of the plantation economy, petty producer agriculture, of both food and cash crops, is important in the Nande region. For example, at the end of 1980 in Beni zone, 'in spite of the existence of large plantations, peasant holdings contributed 85% of coffee production and 90% of Arabica, 38% of tea and almost all the papaya' (ibid: 509). Even in the absence of specific data to show the economic importance of commercial small-scale agriculture since 1985, we can reasonably suppose from the high number of growers (especially for coffee, papaya and cinchona) that it still remains important in the region (see Table 3.4). Tea, for which we do have information, covered a planted area of 460 ha. at the end of 1986 of which 247 ha. belonged to CAK[6] and 216 ha., or about 48%, to petty producers. As we will show (on p. 61), however, in spite of their active participation in commercial agriculture, these small farmers participate less and less in the fraudulent export of their products.

Gold and ivory, two of the most important commodities entering into the transactions of the second economy, are produced according to local regulations.

Gold

In the case of gold, the recent liberalization measures, have given free rein to private initiative. Unemployed youths, organized in small work teams far from home in Kumu, Pere and Lese territory, to the northwest and west of the Nande, devote themselves to the production of gold. They live in semi-permanent mining camps in the forest, with their own social organization, seeking to make profits and live in freedom from the harassment of the civil, military and customary authorities.[7]

These mining camps constitute semi-permanent villages. Gold digging is the major economic activity and shapes all the social relations and the distribution of power within the mining camp. Some farming is carried out in the surrounding area. Leadership roles are usually filled by the founders of the camps, but enterprising individuals are also involved in the exercise of power. These camps average about sixty diggers, young and usually single; those who are married do not have their families with them. They operate in small teams of from six to ten individuals, and competition is intense between teams. After big sales, team members give parties and often return home for a vacation. They call these visits 'landing' (*erikama*), referring to the landing of an airplane after a difficult flight. 'Landing' also connotes financial success: during these vacations the diggers engage in conspicuous consumption, drinking, going on buying sprees, and chasing women. Although some diggers spend all they earn in this way, others save their money to accumulate capital and open small stores.

The camps are protected by local traditional headmen, who share the profit from the mining activities. The camps are inaccessible to the local administration and police because of their geographical remoteness and also because of the aggressiveness of their inhabitants, who quickly turn themselves into an armed force when threatened. These camps have revived the local economy of these isolated regions, depressed since the departure of the M.G.L. mining company. Itinerant traders bring such otherwise unavailable commodities as kitchen salt, soap, cigarettes, clothes and bottled industrial beer, to supply village stores where the miners pay for them with gold.

Gold buyers and sellers recognise a scale of weights and measures of their own, which is current also in East Africa, especially in Kenya, but it is difficult to give the equivalent in standardized international weights. Weights used include a match stick (*musiku*, pl. *misiku*), small coins (*sengi* and *likuta*, pl. *makuta*), a half dollar piece (*dola*), and the *hafu* (probably derived from 'half'). In this system, the amount known as a 'kg.' corresponds to one *likuta* or about 20–25

51

grammes of gold (about 4 carats) in international weights. Equivalences are as follows:

6 match sticks (*misiku*) = 1 sengi
2 *sengi* = 12 match sticks = 1 *likuta*[8]
1 *dola* = 9 *makuta* + 1 *sengi* = 4 *hafu*
1 *hafu* = + 250 g.

It is not surprising that some of these measures have East African English names, since Nairobi is North Kivu's biggest partner in the gold trade.

Ivory
Elephants are hunted in the forest and especially in the country's national parks. Ivory has always been a form of wealth in Nande society: traditionally one tusk could be exchanged for 25 goats; ten goats or one cow were used for bridewealth payments.

Virunga National Park is the best territory in which to hunt elephants in North Kivu. Armed poachers have confronted the park rangers for many years. For the poacher, hunting elephant in the park is lucrative but also dangerous and to give themselves courage, they take drugs, consult with medicine men, and undergo protective rituals before the hunt.

Ritual preparation for elephant hunting in the park consists of a bath in a fast-flowing river. The team of poachers carry out the ritual in silence and naked, which is how they hunt. They wash their entire body, rubbing it with herbs, and magical medicines supplied by specialists. An individual's back must be turned upstream, his stomach downstream. The bath is followed by a meal prepared by the men and taken together in silence. A spear point or hunting knife serves to pass the food. The meal consists primarily of meat, but also of yams, taro and potatoes. It is followed by strong doses of drugs (hemp) before the hunt itself, which is preferably undertaken at night.

Elephant hunting is illegal in Zaire. But ivory is a much sought-after commodity, not only in Zaire but also in the Sudan, Rwanda, Burundi and the West. Elephants are one of the great natural resources of northeast Zaire, but huge numbers are killed by poachers: during the research, a truck loaded with eight tonnes of ivory was seized by the government while parked in Goma. Among smuggled commodities, ivory is the most valuable. It is worth more than gold, or coffee and other export crops; a kilogram of ivory sold for 25,000 Z in 1987.

The Trade in Skins, Live Animals and Other Commodities
Animals with valuable skins are not killed with bullets or spears. They are either stunned with a club or captured alive and strangled with the help of a long post thrust into a bunch of dried grass.

Young lions, leopards, gorillas, chimpanzees and zebras are captured live for eventual sale to zoos in Europe, America or Asia, or as pets. They are taken to Nairobi or Mombasa in Kenya, and sold to Asians who export them, or are sold in Goma and taken straight away to Europe by plane. In March 1987, the price of a young animal varied between 300,000 Z and 500,000 Z.

Other commodities not locally produced, also enter into these trade flows at particular times. They include cigarettes, shoes, and beauty products. In March 1987, for example, the price of cigarettes rose sharply in Butembo, especially Embassy Red (BAT). A shortage had been artificially created by the sub-regional authorities who were fraudulently exporting part of the local supply to the Sudan through the frontier post of Aru/Base, where a case of 50 cartons of cigarettes sold for 50,000 Z, rather than for 18,000 Z in Butembo. Thus a carton of cigarettes costing 370 Z in Lubero/Beni could be sold for 1000 Z in Aru/Base (or at 100 Z the packet instead of 40 Z). With the consequent shortage, the price of cigarettes in Butembo rose from 40 Z to 80 Z the packet, an increase of 100%. The next month the price dropped again to 50 Z.

Forms of Trade

The various forms of unrecorded trade include: private sale for prices which are bargained; smuggling, often by companies and official exporters alongside official export, by means of false declaration of quantity or quality or under- or over-invoicing to avoid customs dues; and barter, especially common in Beni and Lubero during periods when the value of the zaire has fluctuated wildly.

Some of the routes employed for export in the second economy are the same as those for official exports (Beni/Kasindi, Rutshuru/Ishasa, Goma airport etc). Others, however, are specific to the second economy, such as Aru/Base/Sudan, Aru/Liwara/Sudan, Mahagi/Bonjeli/Uganda (see Map 3.3). This multiplicity of export routes serves to open up the region economically.

In the absence of hard currency, vehicles and other goods are bartered directly for local products such as gold, coffee or ivory. Standardized equivalences exist in this trade, as follows:

1 Yamaha motorcycle = 10 kg. ivory = 20 'kg.' gold = 1 tonne coffee
1 pick-up truck = 100 kg. ivory = 200 'kg.' gold = 10 tonnes coffee
1 Mercedes truck = 1 tonne ivory = 800 'kg.' gold = 40 tonnes coffee
1 bicycle = 0.5 kg. ivory = 1 'kg.' gold = 150–200 kg. coffee

Coffee and ivory, because they are heavy and difficult to conceal when crossing the frontier, are exchanged by preference directly for other commodities on the spot or at the markets of Aru/Base, Liwara or Bonjeli. Only the big smugglers export them as far as foreign countries. They do it with the complicity of certain officials. They must include in their expenses bribes for customs officials, who, in such cases, often demand exorbitant amounts.

Local people engage in these forms of unrecorded trade in an attempt to overcome problems in marketing their products in the official system.

Imports

Manufactured goods (food and clothing), construction materials, coffee, vehicles and motorcycles, spare parts and fuel are among the commodities imported into Beni and Lubero, as shown in Map 3.3. Manufactured goods are generally imported from Nairobi, Kenya. In some cases the two modes of importing (official and unofficial) are combined at all stages. Two or three months before the research, a single trader in Butembo had brought to the town thirty-six trailer trucks of merchandise (including radios and cloth) from East Africa. Some of these goods had come from as far away as Japan, Taiwan and Hong Kong, markets which some young traders have discovered and begun to explore.

Older, well-established traders import legally; young unlicensed traders, just starting out and trying to accumulate venture capital, are most often those who smuggle and bribe the customs officials. It is hard to estimate the volume of goods imported illegally in proportion to those imported legally. The banks of Beni and Lubero seldom, if ever, grant foreign exchange to local traders, so since it is well known that these traders import enormous quantities of goods for the local market, one can reasonably assume that most of this importing is done illegally. Another indicator of the scale of imports in the second economy is that, according to local official sources, at the end of 1986 about 860 vehicles and 627 motorcycles were licensed in the Beni-Lubero region; in 1981–1982 there were only 563 and 382 respectively.[9] Two thirds of the vehicles and almost all the motorcycles (especially the Japanese Yamaha) came across the Indian Ocean, via Nairobi or Kigali, or from India, Saudi Arabia or the Sudan via the market of Base/Aru. A recent source of supply for large trucks (Mercedes Benz) for Nande businessmen, is Nigeria, through the Central African Republic or southern Chad, and then to Bondo in Upper Zaire.

Ugandan coffee is smuggled into Beni and Lubero zones but coffee from Upper Zaire is probably not brought into North Kivu through second economy channels: some local companies (such as CAPACO) and some Nande businessmen have deliberately acquired coffee plantations in the coffee-growing regions there. They bring their coffee to North Kivu to take advantage of facilities in the area offered by both the official and the underground economies.

In conclusion, local entrepreneurs in the Beni and Lubero region have initiated new methods of export and import in the second economy. They are added to or combined with official methods. The alternatives they offer contribute to the opening up of the region and are attempts to solve the problem of the absence of legal mechanisms of export and import.[10]

We will now look at the impact of the recent reforms on the flow of unrecorded trade from North Kivu.

The Effect of the 1983 Reforms

The reforms in question are the liberalization of prices, the establishment of official purchase counters for gold and diamonds and the devaluation of the zaire.

Price Liberalization

Price liberalization, as the Zairian media continually emphasize, is not supposed to consist merely of arbitrary price fixing by entrepreneurs. Price control by the state has been abolished but prices are supposed to be determined by negotiation between entrepreneurs, consumers and the authorities.

In northeastern Zaire, including North Kivu, price control has long existed in theory but has been impossible to enforce. The following extract from a 1981–82 report by CECOPANE summarises the situation:

> The effectiveness in this area of the Department of Economy and Industry is questionable. If there is some pretense of an inclination to enforce control in Kinshasa, all such illusions disappear in the interior. Price control over such an extensive area as Zaire is an impossible task.
>
> It is up to the zone authorities to control prices. For the zones of Beni and Lubero no official price list has been put out and the so-called official prices have been little respected: beans were supposed to be sold at 75 *makuta* a kilo, potatoes at 25 *makuta*, but the market price was 50 and 10 *makuta* respectively. However, the mere fact that these prices existed, even if they were not respected, gave the opportunity to officials to fleece any merchant who was not conforming to the regulations; the result was a distortion of the price structure (CECOPANE 1982–83 1: 212).

In North Kivu despite the decree of price liberalization in 1983, price control has not ended. For a brief period of about a year, prices were negotiated to reflect the balance between supply and demand. Thereafter, for reasons frequently deplored in the national media, such as arbitrary pricing, speculation, and the intervention of intermediaries, price control was readopted in Lubero and Beni. Currently the rule applied by the Service of Economic Affairs is that the profit margin of traders must not exceed 25% of the original bill from the wholesaler. Although numerous attempts have been made by officials to enforce the price liberalization measures, the distortion of price structure continues, with the accompanying speculation on the part of local entrepreneurs and the harassment of traders by officials.

Table 3.5 shows the difference between the prices set by the Service of Economic Affairs and prices in the market. In Butembo market alone, where the Service is particularly active, the gap is 10–30% for certain products (manioc flour, plantain bananas, meat, kerosene, palm oil, beer) and 40% for others (beans, charcoal). These differences enable certain Economic Affairs agents to harass the commercial population when they make regular checks on markets and commercial establishments. This service as well as OFIDA are the *bêtes noires* of the commercial population, as their corrupt elements can only be appeased by payments in cash or kind.

The Service of Economic Affairs, ever present even in the most remote rural areas of Lubero and Beni, prevents any real price liberalization. For example, at Kaina (see Map 3.1), 200 km. south of Butembo with 25,000 inhabitants, petty commerce is dying out. Some small traders have moved to the big centers of Butembo and Goma, where they can more easily escape the repressive control of this agency. There at least, they can unite with a large number of others to protest against the harassment they suffer.

OFIDA likewise makes its presence felt in the region. While this is reasonable at the frontier posts, it is not justifiable in centers far from the borders, such as Butembo or Beni. Charges levied, according to current practice in the area, are, for example, 1 million zaires at the border customs post for a trailer truck loaded with goods from East Africa. On arrival in Beni or Butembo, as it unloads, it is again subject to dues levied per unit by the local OFIDA office. 'It would not be so bad', sigh the local traders, victims of this abuse, 'if these taxes actually went into the state's coffers!'

The population suffers because prices rise continually. The Office of Economic Affairs in Butembo, which supervises the two zones of Beni and Lubero, recorded the prices of particular products for the period 1984–1986; its figures, for selected products sold in the two zones, shown in Table 3.5, indicate a price increase of from 50–100%, except for a few products, such as glasses of rice or sugar, manioc leaves and local banana beer, for which the price seems stable. The year 1985 shows a steep increase in the price of foodstuffs because of a six-month drought in North Kivu. This natural calamity fell heavily on a population unaccustomed to long dry seasons in North Kivu's equatorial climate.

Table 3.5 shows that price increases affected not only local products, such as foodstuffs and goods from Zaire's urban markets (beer, laundry soap, palm oil, kerosene, cement), but also imports from East Africa or elsewhere (powdered milk, toilet soap, margarine). Price fluctuation is thus influenced by other factors besides the price liberalization measures. These factors include supply and demand, transportation costs and the inflationary tendencies of the national currency.

Table 3.5   Prices of Selected Products in Lubero and Beni Zones
1984–1987 (in zaires)

Product	Official Controlled Price*				Actual Market Price		
	1984	1985	1986	1987**	1987		
					Kaina	Butembo	Beni
Manioc flour (80 kg. sack)	300	450	500	600	300	700	600
Beans (80 kg. sack)	300	600	500	1000	1500	3000	2500
Potatoes (20 kg. basket)	50	70	80	120	180	120	150
Bananas (stalk)	30	40	45	60	–	60	80
Plantain bananas (stalk)	30	50	60	100	–	130	100
Rice (glass)	5	5	5	5	15	5	5
Rice (50 kg. sack)	800	1000	1500	2500	4000	3500	3000
Manioc leaves (bunch)	2	5	3	5	2	5	5
Meat – pork (1 kg.)	70	75	80	100	75	120	150
– beef (1 kg.)	70	75	80	100	75	120	150
– goat (1 kg.)	70	75	80	100	75	120	150
Kerosene (72 cl. bottle)	25	30	35	50	70	70	50
Palm oil (72 cl. bottle)	25	25	30	50	70	60	50
Powdered milk (small can Nido)	150	150	150	200	250	250	200
Soap powder (small box Omo)	15	15	15	20	40	30	30
Toilet soap (Imperial Leather)	25	30	30	50	60	50	50
Laundry soap (1 cake, Isiro)	5	5	8	10	20	15	15
Cooking salt (1 kg.)	15	20	30	40	40	40	40
Sugar (1 glass)	10	10	10	10	15	15	10
Sugar (500 g. pkt)	25	25	30	30	60	60	50
Charcoal (1 sack)	150	150	200	230	200	350	350
Beer (72 cl. bottle) – Primus	30	30	40	60	70	60	60
– Munich	40	40	50	70	–	70	65
Soft drinks	15	15	15	30	40	35	35
Local beer (72 cl. bottle)	5	5	7	10	5	10	10
Salt fish (per unit)	10	10	10	20	20	30	20
Fresh fish (per unit)	15	15	20	30	20	40	30
Coffee (1 kg.)	70	80	80	65	45	45	45
Papain	500	500	750	450	–	–	450
Roofing iron (1 sheet)				700	800	800	800
Cement (1 sack)	500	500	500	600	900	900	900
Margarine (500 g. can)	60	60	75	100	100	100	100

* Service des Affaires Economiques, Butembo.
** price list for 1987 was still in preparation in April.

North Kivu's Abundance of Goods

Scarcity is not a factor in price fluctuation in the region: the markets of Butembo and Beni are so well stocked from unofficial as well as official sources that they supply not only their own rural hinterland but also neighboring areas, such as Bunia and Ituri in Upper Zaire. From examination of the products traded in the shops, boutiques and markets of Beni and Lubero, it appears that trade in these zones depends for about 60% of its supplies on Zaire's urban centres of Kinshasa, Kisangani or Isiro, and for about 40% on imports from foreign sources such as Nairobi or Kigali. Local food production, on the other hand, supplies almost the whole demand for basic foodstuffs. As a consequence of the flexible entry and exit points mentioned earlier, it appears that in North Kivu the markets are generally well supplied.

Mateso Mande comments on the commercial link of North Kivu to Upper Zaire, in a study of a business quarter of Bunia, and notes that ten Nande traders from North Kivu are among the most important business-men in Bunia: 'Their boutiques have the best displays because as well as the usual consumer goods they include rarer articles of clothing and beauty products' (Mateso Mande 1985: 168). These goods come primarily from the markets of East Africa via Butembo. They are much in demand in other Zairian urban markets, such as Kisangani, Bukavu, Goma and Kinshasa, and are the basis of a lively itinerant trade, principally carried out by women. The quality of the goods they trade is so high and prices so low that they eliminate competition. Table 3.6 compares examples of prices of selected goods for Butembo, Lubumbashi and Kinshasa.

Table 3.6 Comparison of Prices in Butembo and Other Principal Centers in 1987 (in zaires)

Product	Butembo	Lubumbashi	Kinshasa
Woman's sweater	1200	2800	2000
Shirt	600	1300	1000
Child's dress	700	1200	1000
Woman's underpants	80	120	100
Hair straightener	70	150	100
Pomade	80	150	120
Perfume	120	200	150

Similar commercial ties link the two zones of Lubero and Beni with Upper Zaire for supplies of food and agricultural products. 'Many agri-cultural products bought in Bunia's central market come from North Kivu, especially potatoes, bananas, onions, beans and cabbage' (ibid: 169).

Transportation Problems
Problems in transporting products to market seem to have had a greater effect on prices than have the liberalization measures. Currently the con-ditions on major roads, such as the Goma-Ruindi-Lubero-Butembo-Beni artery, as well as of minor roads into the rural areas, are very bad (see Map

3.7). The continual heavy rains, the worn-out machinery of the *Office des Routes*, shortage of fuel, and lack of incentives for the road crews are the main reasons for this deterioration. The traditional authorities in the collectivities have neither the equipment nor the financial means at their disposal to undertake repairs and pay workers. In addition, the contract, negotiated in 1982 by the Catholic bishop of Butembo, between the regional government and private business for maintenance of certain rural networks, has not been renewed. In consequence, the difficulty of transportation and the breakdown of vehicles has given rise to price speculation by distributors in an effort to recoup both the losses on their stocks and the repair costs of their vehicles.

Two recent examples will serve as illustrations. Primus and Munich beer is delivered to the markets of Beni and Butembo from Kisangani. The Ituri bridge, out since January 1987, forces the beer transporters from North Kivu to make a detour via Isiro to regain the Beni-Butembo route, a distance of 1,300 rather than 800 km. As a result, the price of beer in Beni and Butembo markets rose from 40–50 Z the bottle to 70–80 Z. After the bridge was repaired in April, the price fell again to 60–70 Z.

Similarly, at the beginning of February 1987, the price of a ticket for the big bus going daily between Goma and Butembo, a distance of 350 km., was raised to 600 Z. The complete deterioration of a 20 km. stretch (between Bikara and Ndoluma) after torrential rains made it necessary to divert all bus traffic from Butembo 250 km. to Bunia in Upper Zaire. During this disruption, which lasted a month and a half, the mobility of the population, especially traders, was reduced to a minimum. Mail delivery was interrupted for the same period for the zones of Beni and Lubero, because by arrangement between ONPTZ and the bus owners the mail is carried on the bus. Service was reinstated at the beginning of April with a 100% increase in the price of a ticket from 600 Z to 1,200 Z. The risk of damage to vehicles and the increase in the cost of fuel quickly pushed the bus owners to raise the price of a ticket without consulting the local authorities.

Since in general the roads in East Africa are better maintained than the roads in the interior of Zaire, goods coming from Kenya and the Indian Ocean ports tend to be sold at a lower price than those coming from urban centers in Zaire. Certainly their rate of price increase is lower than for goods from interior markets. Table 3.5, for example, shows for the period 1984–87 an increase in price of about 30% for powdered milk, detergent and margarine, and of 50% for toilet soap; all come from East Africa. Beer, soda, and palm oil from Zaire, on the other hand, show an increase of 100% or more.

None of these situations facilitates implementing a policy of liberalization. Instead they encourage the expansion of the second economy and discourage small local importers.

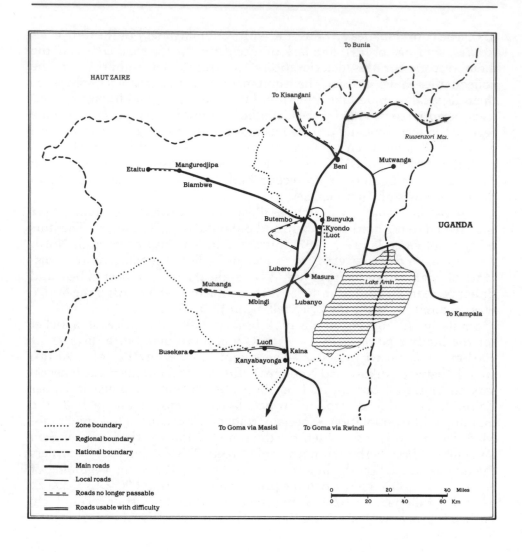

Map 3.7 *Roads of Administrative Zones of Lubero and Beni in North Kivu* (compiled by Vwakyanakazi Mukohya)

Coffee Export: Success for the Reforms

One sector in which price liberalization has had effect is in coffee export. Since 1983, purchase of coffee export documents has been liberalized. The number of official coffee exporters in Lubero and Beni increased from 20 to 34 between 1983–84 and 1984–85, and from 38 to 60 between 1984–85 and 1985–86. At the same time, official coffee exports increased as follows:

1983–84	1,000,000 kg.
1984–85	22,973,940 kg.
1985–86	129,000,000 kg.

Source: OZACAF-Butembo.

Liberalization of official coffee export has brought an increase in the number of buyers in the rural areas. Conditions for obtaining an authorization for buying coffee in the villages and rural areas are possession of a vehicle and payment of an average amount of 1,000 Z a year to OZACAF. Butembo and Beni have experienced a 'coffee rush', especially during coffee harvests. This increase in the number of coffee buyers has contributed to a decrease in smuggling by petty producers themselves. They no longer take their coffee across the frontiers on their backs or by bicycle or by arrangement with truckers, as they have been doing for twenty years. The principal coffee smugglers are now found among the official exporters and authorized buyers owning vehicles. They continue to profit from the situation on the international market to speculate and enrich themselves.

At the time of the research the price of coffee to the producer was very low, 45 Z per kg. instead of the official price of 85 Z per kg. The big producers, such as Brazil, had refused to limit their production and export of coffee, which resulted in the drop in coffee prices on the international market. In the Beni-Lubero region feelings were running high among petty producers, buyers and exporters alike. At the beginning of April 1987, however, a solution was found so that the producer again sold a kilo of coffee for 85 Z: buyers and exporters paid this price in the villages and took the coffee directly to the market of Aru/Base on the Sudanese border, where they bartered it for pickups, trucks and motorcycles. The monetary equivalencies in this exchange were as follows:

1 Yamaha motorcycle = 1 tonne of coffee = 250,000 Z
1 pick-up = 10 tonnes of coffee = 2,500,000 Z
1 Mercedes Benz truck = 40 tonnes of coffee = 10,500,000 Z

In this exchange the clandestine export price of coffee was the equivalent of 250 Z kg., three times the price paid to the producer in the village. For reasons such as this, when the rate of inflation is from 30–40%, barter is preferable as the mode of exchange.

61

Official Purchase Counters for Precious Minerals

Another reform brought about by the liberalization policy of 1983 was the setting up of official counters for the purchase of precious minerals across the country.

In Beni and Lubero, the substances sold are primarily gold, and secondarily cassiterite and wolfram. After the reform, official buyers quickly became known and purchase counters were set up in urban centers and large rural settlements: four in Butembo, three in Beni and two in Kanyabayonga (see Map 3.1).[11] Their local supervisors, however, all from the area but often intermediaries employed by high-level politicians, refused to give any estimate of the quantity of minerals purchased annually. It is said that these counter operators currently consider gold buying as secondary to their other more lucrative activities, such as trade, agriculture or cattle raising, especially since the last fall in value of the American dollar. Gold prices are fixed strictly according to the price on the London market, heard daily on the radio.

Clandestine buyers are numerous and active, some of them even well-known. At the time of the research, a dozen names were mentioned in Butembo alone. Their prices varied between 13,000 Z and 13,200 Z for a 'kg.' of gold (the equivalent of 2,600 Kenyan shillings); official buyers paid only 10,000 Z a 'kg.'

A rough estimate of the quantity of gold entering into Nande businessmen's commercial transactions can be made by calculating the value of the average number of trailer trucks of goods delivered each week. Three of the six largest Butembo traders estimated that four truckloads arrive weekly in Beni and four in Butembo. Local officials in customs, administration and Economic Affairs, with whom this estimate was cross-checked, considered the number to be if anything too low; most trucks come in the night without either control or complicity on the part of the authorities. Most of the goods they bring are obtained in exchange for gold because it is easier to smuggle than the other more bulky commodities exported in unrecorded trade, such as coffee, tea, ivory, papain, and animal skins. These products are generally illicitly traded by those who have influence or power to get the co-operation of the authorities in crossing the frontier.

One truckload of goods is the equivalent (through barter or private sale) of 200–300 'kg.' of gold. At the rate of 200 'kg.' of gold per truck, a conservative calculation, the total quantity of gold entering this trade would be 76,800 'kg.' a year (8 truckloads × 48 weeks × 200) or 1,536,000 grammes (76,800 × 20). This amount is equal to 15,360 kg. of gold in standard international weight. It represents more than seven times the total national production of 1,889 kg. in 1982, twice the 1983 production of 6,001 kg., four-and-a-half times the 1984 production of 3,642 kg., and seven-and-a-half times the 1985 production of 1,957 kg. (production figures from *Conjoncture Economique* 1987: 204).

This trade thus absorbs an enormous proportion of the national gold production. These calculations make understandable the decrease in official production figures, especially from 1983 to 1984, after liberalization, when production dropped by 39%, 'because of smuggling', according to the official annual report put out by the Department of the Economy (*Conjoncture Economique* 1985: 171).

North Kivu's gold functions as a dependable hard currency. It is used by businessmen in markets as far away as Saudi Arabia, Taiwan, Hong-Kong and Japan. Gold smugglers across Zaire's border to Uganda and then to Kenya, hide the gold in the engine or around the wheels of cars. The procedure is that the car is taken to a garage before the trip and again when it arrives in Nairobi. The garage owners are paid for concealing and removing the gold. Businessmen unite in small groups of four or five and commission two to travel in the car. When the goods are delivered by truck from East Africa to Beni or Butembo, they are distributed according to the amount of gold contributed by each participant. Expenses for travel, lodging, food, leisure and any bribes incurred are shared equally among the group. Individuals smuggling small amounts of gold swallow it and abstain from food and drink during the 700–800 km. journey. In Nairobi, they take a laxative, recover their gold and sell it. All those involved in the trade know that the authorities are constantly on the watch for them; the game consists of countering this vigilance, or 'co-operating' if caught.

It seems, therefore, that in North Kivu at least, the establishment of official counters for the purchase of precious minerals has neither prevented them being smuggled or contributed to bringing the revenues they earn into the state's coffers. On the other hand, the policy of liberalizing gold mining has given a new dynamism to the region of North Kivu. Enforcement of preventive legislation in this area could bring about a decline for urban and rural centres, similar to that reported before 1983 for Tshilengi in Kasai Oriental (Lukusa and Tshibanza 1985).

Exchange Rate Adjustments

Between 1983 and 1987, the several devaluations of the national currency had important repercussions in North Kivu.

The most immediate consequences were price rises, especially for petroleum products, roofing iron, and cement. They resulted in a slowing down of the economy in various ways: difficulty in completing construction of houses in durable materials,[12] in repairing national and local roads, and in making provision for inter-urban traffic adequate for the transport of goods and people. Since the last devaluation, traffic between the Nande region and Kisangani has been reduced by about 30% for lack of fuel.

An important consequence in North Kivu of the floating of the zaire is the expansion of the second economy, especially in the import/export sector. As the rate of exchange drops, importers and exporters prefer to keep their money and pay for foreign goods with gold, ivory or coffee. This strengthens the barter economy and favors informal exchange with foreign partners, especially Kenya, Rwanda and the Sudan.

The Effect of Socio-Political Changes in Neighboring Countries on the Flow of Trade from North Kivu

The principal countries with which North Kivu maintains economic exchange relations are Uganda, Kenya (via Uganda), the Sudan, and Rwanda. Kenya and Rwanda have been politically stable, while the Sudan and Uganda are divided internally by political problems, such as the Southern rebellion against the Khartoum government and the factions in the north of Uganda opposing the government of President Museveni. How have these political troubles affected the movement of goods to and from North Kivu?

Uganda maintains few economic ties with North Kivu. Apart from a few products supplied to Zaire, such as empty sacks, hoes (through private sale and smuggling), and fresh fish (bought for the equivalent of 1.20 Z on the Ugandan shore of Lake Amin, instead of 18 Z on the Zairian side), the principal product imported into Kivu is the smuggled Ugandan coffee mentioned above. This flow of coffee to North Kivu is not new: Tanzanian soldiers were heavily involved in this trade at the time of their pacification of Uganda (known locally as the Shaba-Shaba war).

Uganda serves principally as a transit route for businessmen and convoys of goods between North Kivu, Kenya and the Indian Ocean. According to travellers who have used this route, the Ugandan national roads are good, and better maintained than those in Zaire. Likewise, security is fairly good in the southern region of the country crossed by the truck convoys of the Kivu traders. One company, AGETRAF, loads coffee daily at Beni and Butembo during the coffee harvest. Its vehicles, driven by Somalis, cross Uganda and Kenya for the Indian ocean ports, especially Mombasa. No incidents threatening either the drivers or their loads have been reported.

According to current arrangements between Kenyan and Kivu traders, the Kenyans deliver goods, and vehicles in which to transport them, as far as North Kivu. These trucks have 'Transit Goods' written on them in large letters. Very few traders from North Kivu actually travel to Kenya in their own vehicles.

Thus the internal problems and economic breakdown currently afflicting Uganda do not seriously interfere with the flow of exports and imports between North Kivu and the Indian Ocean. This route continues to be an important source of supplies of manufactured and consumer goods, fuel, and spare parts for Kivu.

In the Sudan, Zaire's other trading partner, the rebels opposing the Khartoum government might be expected effectively to block the flow of exports and imports linking the Sudan to North Kivu. But, in fact, Zairian traders and traffickers have never needed to penetrate Sudanese territory for their trade. Those who did so before the war only went to Juba or Khartoum as adventurers in search of new markets. By far the greater part of the trade has always taken place informally in the markets of Base and Liwara in Alur country, still within Zaire's borders. This situation remains unchanged today.

There is one notable difference, however. The markets of Base and Liwara not only make products from the Sudanese market (boutique goods) available to Zairian traders and traffickers, but also those imported into the Sudan from Europe, Saudi Arabia or India (pick-ups, motorcycles, and Indian vehicles made by Tata). Currently, a new category of goods coming from the war, such as vehicles and goods stolen or taken by force, is entering into trade in the markets of northeastern Zaire; all are exchanged through barter for coffee, ivory, tea and food.

Thus here also, socio-political troubles seem to diversify and stimulate rather than hamper exchanges in the second economy. This economy thrives in a troubled socio-economic environment: it is both a reflection and a mechanism of adjustment to such conditions. For North Kivu and northeastern Zaire, the difficulties of neighboring countries are a case of 'the misfortunes of some being the good fortune of others'.

Relations between the Second and the Official Economies

Investigation of the relations between the second and official economies in North Kivu, raises the issue of the implications of the second economy for the development of this region. The concept of 'development' used here is of a global process serving to liberate people from all forms of constraints, permitting them to increase their income and to satisfy their primary needs.

At first sight, the expansion of the second economy and the rush into its activities is a spectacular phenomenon which shocks and amazes the observer. Rural and urban marketplaces are inundated daily with persons of both sexes who buy and sell at prices arrived at by haggling and impossible to control. In Butembo, a rough census of households in the center of town reveals that at least 132 out of 200 sell goods from their houses, in the street, or in one of the eight markets of varying size. A significant number of the young, most of them illiterate, have left their villages to

65

establish themselves permanently in the forest and dig for gold. Poachers, usually also young and better armed than the rangers, ravage the national park of Virunga. According to the park officials at Rwindi, in 1987 there remained no more than about 800 elephants in the park, instead of the 4,000 there were in 1970. Ugandan soldiers, disbanded after the several outbreaks of violence in that country, sell automatic weapons to poachers. Similarly, even official exporters in the region smuggle and fraudulently export coffee, papain, cinchona, tea, etc. They make false declarations of quantity or quality of their products to the customs authorities; they over- or under-invoice and corrupt the agents of OFIDA and Economic Affairs; or they take shelter under the protection of high political officials to enjoy impunity before the law or to escape taxes. Numerous accounts of such activities circulate in the zones of Lubero and Beni, especially in the centers of Butembo and Beni.

All this leaves the observer with the impression of a systematic pillage of the resources of North Kivu and of anarchy in the organization of production, distribution and exchange.

The reasons people participate in the second economy include low salaries, unemployment and the inefficiency of the formal system (MacGaffey 1987: ch. 5); all these circumstances exist in North Kivu, especially in the administrative zones of Lubero and Beni.

UNTZA-Beni estimates, whether correctly or not, about 12,000 wage earners for the zones of Beni and Lubero, for a population of over one million, two-thirds of those employed are in the zone of Beni. In the last ten years, small agricultural industry, wholesale houses and banks have appeared. For example, CAPACO has 723 employees, ENRA 423, SOZADEX 312, PLANOKI 271, NGBA MWANA 213, to give only a few examples. But the vast majority of the Nande population is engaged in commercial agriculture, growing food crops or market gardening. The constraints on them have been described elsewhere (Jurion et al. 1967; CECOPANE 1981–82). They result in low purchasing power for the mass of the population: annual revenue is from $5–800 a head for the richer coffee-growing region in the south (Oicha, Mutwanga, Biambwe, see Map 3.1), but only $130–300 for the rest of the Nande (CECOPANE 1981–82: 657).

The state and its different organizations, which are here understood to comprise the formal system, are omnipresent in North Kivu. A recent official study considered all of the rural collectivities of Lubero and Beni to be effective (*Gouvernorat du Kivu* 1985: 61–65, 70–74). But the state's omnipresence is viewed differently according to whether one is an official of the system, a scientific observer, or a member of the working population. For the first, it indicates efficacity and viability; for the rest, to be effective it must result in the improvement of the conditions of life of the people.

What is striking in North Kivu, is the multitude of private economic and social activities organized outside the official institutional framework.

For example, the center of Butembo with a population of around 100,000 inhabitants, currently has one hospital (Katwa), two small medical centers (Kitatumba and Matanda) and about thirty small dispensaries. All these health centers are private. No-one knows how they supply themselves with medicines. They do, however, provide basic medical care for the population. The situation is no different in the rural areas of Lubero and Beni, where 80% of health services are supplied by private organizations.

Such initiative and direct contact with the rural population by private individuals gives rise, as one might expect, to a certain amount of nervousness on the part of officials. One official report reads:

> It is regrettable that the UNICEF expert in charge of the rural water system puts himself directly in contact with the local population. This attitude leads to the belief that it is UNICEF supplying the assistance in the key zone of Fizi in South Kivu and not the Executive Council. This practice should be discouraged (*Gouvernorat du Kivu* 1985: 82).

The system of production and distribution depends heavily on private initiative; it is the realm in which the second economy flourishes.

Throughout the two zones of Lubero and Beni, almost 2,000 persons of both sexes are registered with the state as engaged in wholesale, retail or itinerant trade.[13] But there are many more clandestine traders unknown to the state, in rural as well as urban centers. They sell under the commercial registration of a third party, trade in gold or export crops, or buy up foodcrops in the rural areas. In the rural areas themselves, persons of both sexes sell foodstuffs, cooked or uncooked, in the little village markets or along the roads.

The exact volume of these activities is difficult to assess because of their seasonal character. But they are of great importance for balancing household budgets. In Butembo, informal petty trade (*erilavalava*) is considered an alternative to farming, wage employment and formal trade, and may be a crucial source of food and income. Traders are successful because of their knowledge of the milieu and its needs, their assessment of local administrative attitudes, and their mobility. Generalizing from a rough survey done in a section of Butembo, some 60% of the population of centers like Butembo and Beni are involved in this sector, if only part time. The situation is similar to that in Mbuji Mayi, where small commercial enterprises offer 18% of the employment in a town where 80% of the active population is unemployed (Karuhije Mbonimba, 1985: 190). In areas where agriculture is the dominant activity of the population, the proportion would be less. The positive aspect of such trade is that it makes up the deficit in household budgets and provides work, even though only temporarily, to those without it.

While clandestine trade impoverishes the state, it brings considerable wealth to people who have no other means of acquiring it. It represents local solutions to local problems. Degree of participation varies according

67

to the type of trade practiced. Wholesalers and semi-wholesalers generally engage in legal trade, but the kind of trade undertaken by retailers varies according to their age. In general, those who are old or who have been in trade since the early days of independence, engage in legal activities, especially if they already have financial capital or own substantial real-estate. It is among young retailers that one finds the most active participants in the second economy. They use gold and ivory as their means of exchange, and explore the trade routes towards the Indian Ocean, Kigali and, most recently, Bondo in Upper Zaire, as well as the markets of Base and Liwara (see Map 3.2). Since they expand the imports and exports of North Kivu they have, however, contributed to opening up the region.

These petty traders are also responsible for setting up various organizations, which are informal but work well. They include systems of credit with very high rates of interest but available for the commercial population who cannot get credit from the local banks and financial institutions; the setting up of tribunals for settling disputes among businessmen, recognised by the Chamber of Commerce (ANEZA), which settle cases concerning prices, theft, non-payment of debts, and even adultery;[14] and formation of rotating credit groups, like the *likelemba* of western Zaire, which are used especially by women traders whose capital is still small.

The entry into retail and market commerce of Nande women is conspicuous in North Kivu, especially in the centers of Butembo and Beni. They have come to control an increasing share of household income, especially when the head of the household is unemployed or farming unsuccessfully. This situation is bringing about changes in the traditional system of marital authority, upkeep of the household and care of children.

We will end by emphasizing the zeal, sometimes embarrassing to the local administration, with which the businessmen of Beni and Lubero have contributed to public services in the face of the bad management and chronic lack of means of local government. The list of projects is long and we will mention only a few.

Businessmen co-operated in an attempt to set up a hydroelectric plant near Butembo, sufficient to supply Butembo and Beni. Although over ten million zaires were raised, the project has remained on hold since 1978, and even seems to have been abandoned. It is more likely that electricity will eventually be supplied from the center of Ruzizi, near Bukavu. This problem has aroused great impatience and anxiety among the population, since electrification is considered to be one of the most crucial issues in North Kivu.

Road maintenance is another area in which businessmen have become involved, sometimes coming into conflict with the *Office des Routes*. They have had a part in almost all work on the road system of Butembo, since the city authorities have neither the capacity nor the funds to do it themselves. A number of construction projects have also been organized by businessmen, and funded by local subscription, including the new 150-bed

Catholic hospital of Butembo. Local businessmen have also helped in construction of primary schools and financed most of the official visits of political notables.

Through the second economy, new structures of production, distribution and exchange have come into being. These are sometimes parallel, sometimes complementary to the structures of the official economy. The second economy thus contributes in its fashion to the solution of local problems, both collective and individual, and to the accumulation of wealth. Even if it appears to deprive the state of precious resources, it returns them to society in many ways.

Conclusion

The research results, despite the difficulty of collecting data, yield some sort of profile of the import and export sector of the second economy in the zones of Lubero and Beni. As we have emphasized, when the second economy attains the proportions it is assuming in North Kivu, it is because the population is struggling desperately to fill gaps left by the official system; it must be seen as an attempt to challenge hardship and oppression.

In North Kivu the cultivation of food crops in which most of the population is engaged, is not sufficiently profitable. It is subject to various constraints: low producer prices, decline of soil fertility, inadequate infrastructure, scarcity of technical expertise, lack of fertilizer, etc.[15] Commercial agriculture, important as it is in the region, is hardly more profitable. Fluctuation in producer prices and lack of an adequate infrastructure constitute major problems. Thus improved commercialization of agricultural products seems to be one of the most urgent problems to address in the region. CECOPANE, a development project of the Canadian government, identified it as a major problem and attempted systematic experiments with marketing foodstuffs between 1975 and 1980:

> If the results of these pilot projects were not conclusive, they did, however, confirm that the success of any agricultural development program in the northeast (of Zaire, including Lubero and Beni) was closely tied to the setting up of an adequate structure of commercialization.[16]

But their development project in Beni and Lubero for the commercialization of foodcrops has not been followed up.[17]

Development of the commercialization of agriculture is only possible with well-maintained roads. The proper upkeep of the roads in North Kivu would contribute to breaking the economic isolation of this region by providing regular links with national urban centers.

The entire population cannot live through agriculture, however. It is also necessary to create employment opportunities outside it. One solution would be to set up small manufacturing enterprises treating local products. Beni, with enterprises such as CAPACO, ENRA, SODAFI PLANOKI, IPAKI, already provides a good example, even though their orientation is strongly capitalistic and sometimes cumbersome. Small food-processing firms could be established in Beni and Lubero, for example, for canning the abundance of vegetables produced in the market-gardening region of Kyondo-Luotu, and for producing tomato concentrate (currently imported), especially since a small hydroelectric plant has already been set up in the area with Italian aid. To the south, in Beni, jam factories for pineapples, plums and papaya could be established.

The conclusion to all this is clear: the population of Beni and Lubero would devote itself less to using local resources in the activities of the second economy if other means could be found for improving the conditions of life. If alternatives existed, the second economy would cease to be considered, as it currently is, as the sure means outside the meagre opportunities offered by agriculture, wage employment and legal commerce, to acquire wealth and improve living conditions.

Notes

1. Translated and edited by Janet MacGaffey.
2. It has recently been the subject of several research studies, see Vwakyanakazi 1982, Mubake 1984, and MacGaffey 1987.
3. UNTZA-Beni gives about 12,000 salaried workers in the two zones of Beni and Lubero at the end of 1986.
4. According to OZACAF, Butembo.
5. Foreign-owned plantations were supposed to be handed over to Zairians in 1974. Many were neglected and abandoned and were to be handed back to their former owners, according to the Decree of Retrocession of 1976 (ed.).
6. CAK began as a tea project of the European Common Market around 1970. It was privatized in 1983 and management contracted out to BURESMA (groupe DAFOR). The following figures show that privatization has resulted in an increase of production.

Tea Production at Butuhe, Butembo, in kg.

1977	91,764	1982	292,555
1978	225,139	1983	270,724
1979	250,446	1984	399,927
1980	312,925	1985	576,775
1981	359,221	1986	722,910

Source: CAK-Butuhe, Butembo.

7. I have described their organization in 1980 (Vwakyanakazi 1982: 332–35); it continued the same in 1987.
8. All these measures are in terms of weight. *Likuta* (pl. *makuta*) and *sengi* are small coins. The weight of two *sengi* is equivalent to that of one *likuta*. According to informants, traders dislike weighing *dola* against *sengi* because too many pieces of *sengi* would be needed in the balance.
9. Source: *Brigade Routière* and CECOPANE vol. 1, p. 98.

70

10. I have explained in my dissertation that this process of innovation among local small traders in eastern Zaire comes from imitation and apprenticeship through trial and error, and has its roots in the colonial period. It is one of the principal characteristics of what is currently known as entrepreneurship (Vwakyanakazi 1982: ch. 2)
11. A village that was formerly a center for the illegal gold trade (ed).
12. One hundred were left unfinished in Butembo, also two churches, a Catholic hospital and a private nursery school, and thirty houses in Beni.
13. According to the reports of ANEZA, Butembo.
14. These tribunals seem to be declining in importance and litigation tends to be referred to ANEZA, apparently because of the frequent changes in the committees running ANEZA and the upward mobility of some of those who started these organizations.
15. Details are given in the report 'Production Vivrières. 5. Campagne 1984-85,' *Gouvernorat du Kivu.*
16. Project CECOPANE, *Mission au Zaire*, Sept. 1982, p. 8.
17. See *Rapport CECOPANE*, 1981-82, Vol. IV.

4

Unrecorded Trade in Southeast Shaba and Across Zaire's Southern Borders[1]
RUKARANGIRA WA NKERA & BROOKE GRUNDFEST SCHOEPF

This chapter explores activities that take place on the margins of the law, or 'underground', in Southeast Shaba and across its borders. Intensive field study was carried out by the first author in March and April, 1987. The objectives were to discover who does what and how in this trade; the means traders use to avoid the authorities; how unrecorded trading activities are integrated into, or linked to, the 'official economy' which is regulated and taxed by the state, and to determine the effects on it of the economic stabilization measures of 1983. This data and in-depth interviews are used to analyse connections between individual survival strategies, wider social networks and the macrolevel political economy.

Unrecorded trade takes place within Shaba itself, with other regions of Zaire, and across the border by truck to Zambia or by air to South Africa, Europe and the Far East. Unrecorded trade includes trafficking in minerals, spare parts, fuel, stolen cars, foodstuffs, pharmaceuticals, manufactured goods, and sacks for maize, as well as the sale of foreign currencies, and poaching. These clandestine activities are carried on in the Shaba copperbelt cities of Lubumbashi, Kolwezi, and Likasi, and in certain towns and villages on the Zambian border. The study focuses on small-scale fraud[2] at the frontier town of Sakania, on the sale of stolen Zambian cars in Lubumbashi, on the trade in fuel stolen from GECAMINES, the large national copper mining company, and on poaching in Upemba National Park. The flow of these commodities is shown on Map 4.1.

The first step was to compile an inventory of all unrecorded trade in Shaba around the copperbelt towns. Feasibility, time and funds determined the focus on particular activities. The field study, using participant-observation, lasted five weeks. Considerable data were acquired in a short time by focusing on activities in which the fieldworker could make use of contacts and networks established in the course of previous research on-going since 1981.[3] During the field study, Dr Rukarangira shared the life of traffickers, observing their activities and conversing with them. He travelled by train, bicycle, and on top of trucks. He ate at the side of the road and slept in 'bush hotels'. He shared in all the hardships of travel on

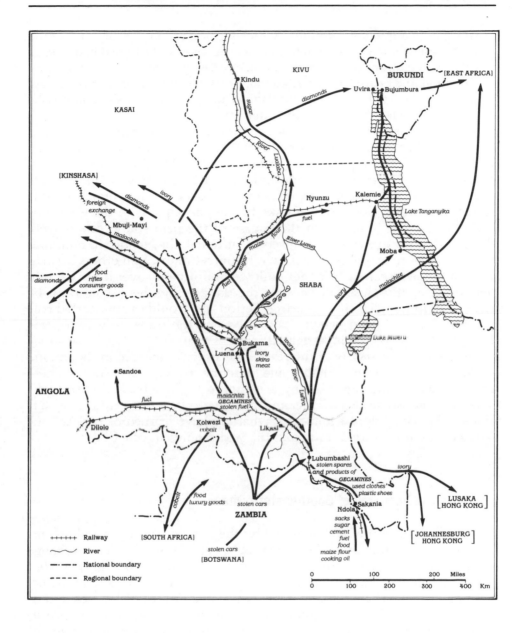

Map 4.1 *Principal Commodities of Unrecorded Trade in S.E. Zaire*
(compiled by Janet MacGaffey)

local roads in appalling condition, which worsen immeasurably during the rainy season when the research took place. Above all, he joined in drinking with his companions of the road. A journey being a liminal period, a time-out-of-time, the researcher profited from privileged moments of relatively intimate contact with strangers, during which shared hardships and risks constituted a temporary basis of fraternity.

The field worker was able to move into the different milieux by travelling as a prospector for a businessman with money to invest, or as a salesman wishing to enlarge the scope of his activities. He also participated by getting himself hired to load and unload trucks of smuggled goods. He found out prices and current practices by observing and comparing different operations. Some of the risks to the participants in these various activities became apparent in the course of the field study; others were described by the individuals themselves, although they tended to minimize them in order to emphasize their own resourcefulness. Still others became known to the researchers as they followed informants over time. Certain networks, tightly closed because of the dangers involved, could not be entered during such a short research period, nor could the purported role of politically powerful persons taking part in the trade, to which some informants alluded, be investigated.

Following an overview of the regional economy centered in the mining region of southeastern Shaba, we describe trading activities.[4] These descriptions are then 'peopled' by excerpts from three traders' narratives. They indicate some of the risks and benefits to be gained from irregular trade. The conclusions summarize what we have learned of connections between the unrecorded trade and the wider political economy.[5]

The Economy of Southeastern Shaba

The regional economy is dominated by the mining of copper and cobalt. The mining sector provided some 80% of Zaire's foreign exchange earnings in 1987; 65% came from copper (*Economist Intelligence Unit* 1989). The high-grade copper ores also contain cadmium, gold and zinc, germanium, molybdenum and other space-age metals. Yellow-cake uranium ore used in the first atomic bombs may once again become profitable. Shaba's mineral wealth is important to the national economy and of strategic importance to the Western powers as well. While dependence on mining makes Zaire's economy vulnerable to price fluctuations beyond its control, the existing productive capacity is too valuable to be allowed to decay; its maintenance requires continued investments in technology and infrastructure.

GECAMINES (GCM), the parastatal successor to the Belgian colonial *Union Minière du Haut Katanga*, employs about 36,000 workers. As

Zaire's largest employer and source of government revenues, it is the determining element in the regional economy. The balance between food prices and wages is of concern to both GCM and regional authorities who seek to avoid strikes and general urban unrest (Schoepf interviews 1975, 1981, 1985).

Lubumbashi and the other cities of southeastern Shaba have grown rapidly because of the rural exodus consequent upon neglect of agriculture and the declining terms of trade for peasants' staple produce. The urban population probably has doubled since 1973 and currently totals between 1.2 and 1.5 million. The stagnation of copper mining for fifteen years has contributed to a regional economic crisis and to unemployment. The vast majority of adults are without waged jobs, while most informal sector occupations are poorly remunerated (Muyayalo 1976; Schoepf 1978/81).[6] Foodstuffs are persistently scarce, despite the various development projects that have attempted to remedy the situation since 1973: maize production in Shaba is insufficient to meet even local demand; moreover, part of the harvest is sent to eastern Kasai, where prices in the diamond-mining area are higher still (Schoepf and Schoepf 1984; Schoepf 1984, 1985a, 1987; Newbury and Schoepf 1989). Smuggled food from Zambia is crucial to supplying the copperbelt cities and the Kasai diamond-mining area. Food prices are higher in Zaire than in Zambia due to government subsidies in the latter country and because of scarcity in Zaire.

Informants point to the arbitrary nature of the boundaries between Zaire and Zambia and the fact that rural dwellers living on both sides of the border are members of the same ethnic group with relatives in both countries. Indeed the curious shape of the boot of Shaba is an artefact of the late nineteenth-century scramble for mineral rights by competing Belgian and British-based interests. During the colonial period people moved back and forth to avoid whichever colonial impositions were experienced as most onerous at the time (Schoepf 1987). This perspective legitimizes a local view of the international boundary as an artificial construction to be taken lightly. An account of the vigorous transborder trade that flourishes in this region begins with a description of the smuggling of foodstuffs from Zambia to Zaire.

Smuggling Through Sakania

Sakania lies 200 km. southeast of Lubumbashi and 18 km. north of Ndola, the principal town of the Zambian copperbelt. It is connected to Lubumbashi by a road which is paved only for half the distance, as well as by rail. At least three-quarters of the goods which come from Zambia to Shaba pass through this frontier post, and about half of these are essential products which sustain the inhabitants of the Zairian copperbelt.

The Kenia marketplace of Lubumbashi is in large part supplied by Zambian goods which also find their way to the Central Market and retail shops. Trucks to Zambia leave daily from this market around eleven o'clock in the morning. A place in one cost 200 zaires in February 1987. The second half of the journey is very rough going, because of the deterioration of the road, especially in February, after five months of heavy rains. The driver stops at nightfall because the road is so bad, and passengers spend the night in the truck. Setting out at daybreak, they arrive at their destination the next evening. In addition to the advantageous prices of goods purchased in Zambia, often from government-subsidized supplies, the trade is attractive because of massive unemployment among Zairians whose labor is thus without opportunity cost.

In Zambia, the population of Ndola, the most important industrial and administrative center of the Copperbelt Province, has increased in size rapidly because of the recent rural exodus. While peasant farming is poorly remunerated, urban unemployment is estimated at 50% of the adult male population (Kydd 1988). The inability of the formal economy to absorb all those seeking work has given rise to shantytowns of the unemployed and a large population in need of ways to make money in the informal sector. In spite of the flight to the towns, Zambia continues to produce plentiful supplies of maize for the domestic market, in part due to the costly policy of subsidizing both production and marketing.

Maize was formerly purchased by a government marketing board; liberalization in 1986 introduced a chain of intermediaries who collect the maize harvest. The grain is sold to large milling companies at subsidized prices. These in turn sell flour to traders at prices fixed by the government. Ndola also has an oil refinery and wholesale outlets for factories that produce sugar and cooking oil. Subsidies on all these products maintain the purchasing power of waged workers and the urban unemployed. The threat of tampering with food subsidies led to demonstrations in Zambian cities in December 1986. All products fetch higher prices across the frontier in Zaire:

In southeastern Shaba, as a direct consequence of unemployment, inadequate salaries, and the scarcity of essential goods since 1974, a category of people known as 'traffickers' (*trafiquants*) has emerged. These people, of whom smugglers are a sub-category, are increasingly numerous. Some of them appear to possess considerable wealth, and they include a growing number of the educated, including university graduates unable to find professional employment. The two features that Lubumbashi shares with Ndola and that are the key to smuggling are, first, the large number of unemployed and, second, the complicity of some customs agents, the military and the police, who take advantage of opportunities to supplement their salaries. Informants assert that officials *mangent à la chaine*, meaning that some higher-level officials obtain a share of the bribes paid to their subordinates. They say that this 'chain' exists on the Zambian side of the border as well, although until 1975 officials had a reputation for probity.

Organization of the Smuggling Trade

The products smuggled, in order of importance, are:

To Zaire: maize flour, sugar, cooking oil, fuel, empty sacks (during the maize harvest), and miscellaneous products.

To Zambia: bales of imported used clothing, plastic shoes (manufactured by SOZAPLAST, the *Société Zairoise de Plastique*, and spare parts and other items stolen from GECAMINES.

The social organization of smuggling includes five categories of people who are involved in fraud at the frontier.

Buyers. The buyers are the traffickers who own the capital and order the goods from the transporters and suppliers, either Zairian or Zambian. They stay in Zaire to receive and pay for the goods sent by the smuggler/suppliers who do the direct buying. The latter pay the transporters. The level of education of these buyers appears to be rising over time. Buyers report that in order to have staying power and avoid complications it is necessary to have friends in high places.

Transporters. The transporters carry the goods between the buyers and the suppliers. The great majority are Zairians living in Zambia; most of them living there illegally. Some use their own bicycles, but most rent them from Zambians and earn their living riding them loaded with goods for smugglers along bush paths. It is hard and risky work but much more profitable than hoe agriculture. Some transporters also play the role of the smuggler-suppliers. If they have a little money, they receive orders from Zaire, make purchases with their own money in the stores, and stock and load their delivery themselves.

Suppliers. The suppliers are mostly Zambians who have stores, and consequently have obtained purchasing quotas from the sugar and oil mills. They make arrangements with the Zairian buyers who want large quantities, selling to them at a higher price than the legal one fixed by the state.

Officials. Certain corrupt elements among the military and police authorities allow the transporters to pass, and protect them, after receiving payment for all items of merchandise. Some customs officials profit from arrangements they make with the traffickers, who underdeclare their goods and share the customs fees due on what is declared.

Smugglers-Suppliers. Most of the smugglers are Zairians who live in Zambia without residence papers. They live especially in certain shantytowns, where they stock the goods bought from the wholesalers. These goods are transported 15 km. to one of the villages on the Zairian border which, in order to protect informants, we will call 'Frontier Village'. In this village there is a market at which the Zambian goods are sold. Buyers and transporters come from Lubumbashi to this village and take the smuggled goods to Lubumbashi and the first customs post.

This trade is not haphazard, but institutionalized; it operates according to rules known to all participants. Profits vary according to commodity.

Maize Flour

Maize is the preferred food staple of Shaba and Kasai. Maize flour smuggled from Zambia makes up for insufficient local supplies, and constitutes a significant addition to the official imports from southern Africa. One unpublished report estimated that some sixty thousand tons were smuggled from Zambia in 1985–86. This was about one-third of the region's requirements, but much of it was shipped on to Kasai, where prices are higher.

Zambian maize flour comes in three grades, the second grade being the one preferred in Shaba. The retail price is 28.80 kwacha (K)[7] for a 50 kg. sack, but smugglers will pay 30 K. A smuggler buys a large quantity, stocks it, then gets in touch with his contact in the Zambian military to arrange its passage. He pays the soldiers 5 K a sack and pays an additional 10 K per bicycle-load to Zairian soldiers across the frontier. The transporter gets 10 K per sack; a bicycle in good repair can transport four sacks and make three trips a day. The buyer who engages the transporters also hires a guard for each convoy of bicycles for protection against thieves. The path to the frontier goes through the bush, by-passing the Zambian frontier post. The goods are taken to the warehouse designated by the buyer in Frontier Village in Zaire.

In February 1987, a supplier who came to buy at Frontier Village paid 55–60 K[8] for a 50 kg. sack. This price included the 30 K purchase price, an additional 10 K for transportation, 7.5 K for bribes, and a 16% profit of 7.5 K. This came to 60 Z per sack, at the parallel exchange rate of 8 zaires to 1 kwacha. A transporter carrying four sacks a trip for 40 K, made 120 K a day, making three trips daily. Deducting 10 K for renting the bicycle he could thus earn 110 K or 880 Z in one day. At the time this was equivalent to about $8; two-thirds of the monthly minimum wage and one-fifth the *monthly* salary of a mid-level government employee.

On average about 1,500 to 2,000 sacks of maize flour cross the border each day in this way, an indication of the scale of this form of smuggling and of the amount of money it brings to the military on both sides of the frontier. This trade is carried on quite openly by day. It can also be done clandestinely at night, thus avoiding payments to both the Zambian and the Zairian military. But if the clandestine transporter is caught, everything he carries, as well as his bicycle, is confiscated. Most people thus prefer to work during the day, which while less lucrative is also less risky.

78

Sugar

Although sugar is produced in Zaire on plantations in the regions of Kivu, Haut Zaire and Bas Zaire, domestic supplies are insufficient to meet ever-increasing demand. Most of domestic production is sold in Kinshasa, while Shaba and Kasai import from South Africa, Zambia and Malawi, generally through the big import houses. However, sometimes there are scarcities because of the shortage of foreign exchange; smuggled sugar then fills the demand. There is, however, some smuggling at all times because Zambian smuggled sugar is cheaper than sugar legally imported from South Africa.

A Zairian smuggler buys from the Zambian wholesaler at 40 K for a 20 kg. bag (4 K over the official price). A transporter can take a maximum load of 10 bags on a bicycle. The smuggler pays the transporter 5 K for each bag, or 50 K a trip. He must also pay off the military, at the rate of 2 K per bag to the Zambians and 1 K to the Zairians. The sale price at Frontier Village for a 20 kg. bag is 55–60 K, so at 55 K the smuggler's profit is 7 K (15%) a bag, or 56 Z, that is 560 Z per bicycle-load. A transporter making 50 K a trip and three trips a day, and paying 10 K for the rent of his bicycle, makes 140 K or 1,120 Z a day.

The percentage of profit on capital invested is a little lower on sugar than on maize flour, but sugar can be carried in larger quantities (by weight) because of its lesser volume. Thus the trader with sufficient capital can earn considerably more money per day.

Cooking Oil

Oil is the most profitable of all the commodities smuggled, for all the participants involved. Shaba oil mills do not produce sufficient quantities to satisfy local demand, their oil is of lower quality than the Zambian product, and the price is higher. The most widely available oil is palm oil from Bandundu, or from Maniema in Kivu. However, delays on the railways frequently disrupt supplies. In any case, the middle class in Lubumbashi mostly prefer the highly refined Zambian sunflower seed oil to strong-tasting palm oil; the smuggling trade ensures that it is always readily obtainable.

The Zambian oil factory outlet sells barrels of 120 liters (l.), which are divided into 5 l. or 2.5 l. containers. A smuggler buys them for 40 and 20 K respectively. He pays the transporter 2 K to carry each 5 l. container; a maximum bicycle-load is 45 containers. He pays the Zambian military 20 K, the Zairian 15 K, per bicycle-load. He sells 5 l. in Frontier Village at 55 K. His profit is 12.23 K or 92 Z, that is 28%. He thus gets 4,320 Z per bicycle-load, and bicycles generally travel in convoys. The transporter earns 90 K a trip from the Ndola shantytown to Frontier Village. He pays 10 K rent for a bicycle and working intensively, can make three trips a day, so he makes 260 K or 2,080 Z in one day.

Fuel

The supply route for petroleum fuels coming from Matadi to Shaba by the national river and railway system is very long and is subject to frequent delays that result from the shift from rail to boat at Kinshasa and from boat back to rail transport up-river at Ilebo. Supplies are thus uncertain. The quality of Zambian fuel is superior, especially for diesel oil, which is more highly refined than in Zaire. Prices are lower in Zambia, especially in the shantytown of Mandondo around the refinery.

A smuggler pays 280 K for a barrel of kerosene or diesel, 450 K for gasoline. It is transported in a rented truck to the departure point for the frontier and divided into 20 l. containers. The transporter carries ten containers at a time on a bicycle. In the rains when the paths are muddy, he takes a small boy along to help push the bicycle out of the holes. The smuggler pays a transporter 40 K for 200 l. of fuel, and he pays 30 K per bicycle load to the military on each side of the border. At Frontier Village in March 1987, he could sell a barrel of diesel or kerosene for 450 K (3,600 Z), and gasoline for 680 K (5,440 Z). He made a profit of 70 K (560 Z) or 18.5% on diesel or kerosene, and of 130 K (1,040 Z) or 6% on gasoline. The transporter earned 120 K; subtracting 10 K for renting the bicycle, he made 110 K or 880 Z a day. Sometimes the transporter is himself the smuggler and in that case he then sells the fuel directly. Otherwise he fills barrels in a depot as ordered.

Since 150 to 200 barrels or more are filled each day, especially during the maize harvest, the scale of payoffs earned by dishonest elements in the military is enormous. They are, in fact, so large that Zambian soldiers report that they must pay 1,000 K a day to the major who assigns them to this post.

More diesel and kerosene than gasoline are smuggled, in spite of their lower rate of profit, because of increasing demand from the growing number of trucks in Zaire. During the maize harvest especially, the demand for diesel increases noticeably. Many traffickers come to buy it and after passing through customs they transport it by train to Nyunzu, Kitenge and Kongolo in northern Shaba (see Map 4.1). This supply of smuggled fuel makes it possible to collect the maize harvest, since it compensates for the breakdowns of official supplies over long periods.

Miscellaneous Products

These include chickens, eggs, empty sacks, soap powder, toilet paper, biscuits, toothpaste, etc. Transport costs vary according to the type of goods, their quantity and their fragility. The price is negotiable.

Transporters frequently return with empty trucks from Lubumbashi, but they may take plastic shoes and bales of used clothes, as well as small quantities of palm oil for the Zairian community in Zambia. These goods sometimes cross the Zairian frontier fraudulently, but the transporters prefer to declare them to the Zambian customs because their controls are stricter than the Zairian ones, especially for Zairians who do not have import licenses. Those who attempt to slip past the post risk confiscation of their goods if they are caught.

Transport Costs Between the Frontier and Lubumbashi

Goods bought at Frontier Village can be brought to Lubumbashi by train or by truck. Small-scale traffickers, who do not have access to large amounts of capital and thus purchase small quantities of goods, use trucks. To use the train it is necessary to have at least 30 tonnes in order to fill a railway wagon. These wagons are rented individually: it is preferable to rent a whole wagon at a time because then it can be sealed against theft. If the same one is used by many people there is risk of theft. Truck transport is very expensive, taking into account payments for avoiding the customs and police. The truck driver deals with all these matters while the trafficker takes the train which gets to Lubumbashi the same day. Due to the poor state of the road, the journey by truck takes two to three days. Transport fees are usually paid in the Kenia market in Lubumbashi after the goods are sold, though the customers must be people whom the transporter knows well and can count on not to delay payment.

The transporter uses passenger fares and freight charges to pay the customs and other authorities. The single fare per person is 300 Z in each direction. Freight charges are as follows:

Lubumbashi – Sakania	zaires
Bale of used clothing	150
Empty barrel	100
Consignment of plastic shoes	100
Sakania – Lubumbashi	
Sack of maize flour (with customs)	200
Barrel of fuel (with customs)	1,300 (without) 100
20 kg. bag of sugar	160
Cooking oil per container (with customs)	118 (without) 70
Empty sacks/100	2–300

The customs agent at Frontier Village is supposed to inspect loads in order to levy dues, but often the transporters load up at night, arrive very early in the morning in large numbers, and in the confusion are allowed to make their own declarations. Taxes are imposed not only by customs but also by the zone, by the *Office Zairois de Contrôle* (OZAC) and the Anti-Fraud Brigade.[9]

A number of ruses have been developed for evading customs dues. One common way to reduce customs charges is for the transporter to under-declare the quantity of his goods. For example, if he has 20 barrels of diesel he will declare 5 to be diesel and 15 to be kerosene and thus pay 1,500 Z less than he should, or he will declare bales of 100 sacks to consist of only 50, or 15 container cartons of cooking oil to contain only 10, thus saving 33% of the customs dues.

Another ruse is to load the truck in such a way as to disguise the real contents. For example, barrels of kerosene and diesel will be loaded at the sides, sacks of maize flour and empty sacks on top, and in the center will be a space filled with sacks of sugar and containers of cooking oil (see sketch in Fig. 4.2), both of which have a higher tax rate but they will not be declared and so the assessed rate for the load will be lower than it should be.

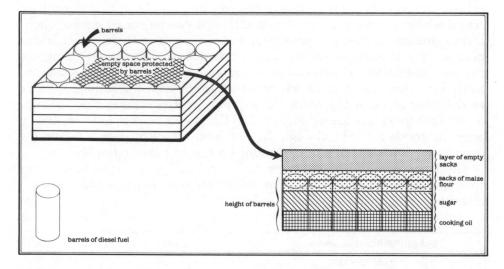

Fig. 4.2 *Method of Loading Truck for Smuggling Goods*
(compiled by Rukarangira wa Nkera)

Finally, smugglers may make arrangements with particular customs officials. Thus, for example, the transporter underdeclares the value of a ten-ton truck loaded with cooking oil, so that out of 1,340 containers he evades paying dues on 670, saving 32,160 Z. The customs official calculates that he owes 64,320 Z and inquires if he will pay or come to an 'arrangement'. For an arrangement the official writes down only half the load, assessing duties to the value of 32,160 Z. The value of the other half is divided between them: the official gets 16,080 Z and the transporter saves the same amount. Altogether the latter pays 48,240 Z in dues, considerably less than he should; the state coffers are made 32,160 Z lighter by this collusion.

Once the arrangement has been made, the customs official gives the transporter a receipt for 32,160 Z to go with the document that states the vehicle's load and registration number. He takes this document to the authorities at Sakania, pays dues, and gets a receipt. The same strategy is employed with the authorities of the zone and with OZAC. Then comes the Anti-Fraud Brigade. Documents are never shown to officials who are being corrupted. The transporter simply states the amount of his load as half what it really is, and pays a bribe to avoid inspection. The final barrier is the military: here each trucker hands over either a sack of maize flour or 500 Z. At 110 km from Lubumbashi there is a customs post for checking documents; if the officials want to verify anything they are paid a little money and they then initial the document. Any further controls are dealt with in the same way.

The rate of profit on commodities sold in the Kenia market in Lubumbashi and obtained through this trade with Zambia is shown in Table 4.3. Transporters report that their profits are 50,000 Z minimum per round trip after expenses. They say they average six trips a month. If so and if all goes well on each trip, they can make 300,000 Z a month. This does not include depreciation of the truck, spare tires, maintenance repairs etc. However, since many trucks are stolen and cost only 800,000 to 1,000,000 Z each, the cost of a truck can be recovered in a relatively short period, four to five months of intense activity, provided that one has sufficient capital to invest.

Table 4.3   Profits on Commodities Sold in Kenia Market Feb-March 1987
(Prices in kwacha and zaires)

Goods	Purchase Price at Frontier	Transport and Payoffs	Storage and Handling	Total Cost	Sale Price	Profit	%
Maize flour 50 kg. sack	55 K	25 K 200 Z	12.5 K 100 Z	740 Z	1,000 Z	260 Z*	35
Sugar	55 K 20 kg.	20 K 20 kg.	32 Z kg.	32 Z kg.	40 Z kg.	8 Z kg.	25
Cooking oil 5 l	55 K	8.75 K	20 Z	530 Z	600 Z	70 Z†	13
Diesel & kerosene	450 K	162.5 K 1,300 Z	25 K 200 K	5,100 Z	6,500 Z	1,400 Z	27
Empty sacks							
90 kg.	24 Z	7 Z	3 Z	34 Z	70 Z	36 Z	10
100 kg.	32 Z	7 Z	3 Z	42 Z	80 Z	38 Z	90

* Flour is still more profitable if it comes by train, since it costs 88 Z instead of 200 Z by truck.

† Profits on oil are lower than those on other commodities, but it is much more profitable because of the large quantities that a truck can transport, when only a third will be declared, or, depending on how the truck is loaded, maybe none at all.

The Effects of Liberalization

'Liberalization' or the removal of price controls on some primary products and consumer goods has had several effects on the region's irregular trade. Liberalization of artisanal gold and diamond mining has affected Shaba indirectly. This reform decree resulted in a diamond rush in Kasai, followed by a decline in local agricultural production and a scarcity of foodstuffs in the markets. The rise in food prices that ensued, especially of the basic staple of maize flour, has increased the number of traffickers coming from Kasai to Shaba to buy maize flour, cooking oil and even eggs. Others come to change their zaires to dollars in Lubumbashi. They use dollars to import cement legally from Zambia, which they transport by rail to Kasai, in response to the expansion of the construction business that has followed the diamond rush. One result of this 1983 reform for Shaba, therefore, has been circulation of the money earned in diamonds in Kasai to Shaba, and an increase in both legal and fraudulent imports into Shaba from Zambia destined for Kasai.

The effect of price liberalization on local maize production in Shaba has been mixed. Regional authorities, worried about the impact of high prices on urban political stability, were reluctant to remove controls.[10] At first, higher prices constituted an incentive for peasant producers.[11] Then devaluation in September 1983 meant that cultivators had to pay five times as much as previously for consumer necessities, fertilizer and hybrid seeds. Peasants complained that they were no better off than before.[12] When maize prices sky-rocketed prior to the 1984 harvest, official producer price ceilings were reintroduced.[13] The resulting loss for small producers was considerable (cf Schoepf, 1985a,b, 1987; Schoepf et al. in press b). In some places, the nutrition of peasant households suffered as larger fields were planted to maize to maintain cash incomes.[14] Young children suffered most. Traders reported that they were doing well, however (see below). While regional maize production has increased since 1985, price policy is only one element in a complex situation. Incentives to large and medium-scale producers in the form of land titles and subsidized credit are another element. Increased administrative coercion of small village cultivators is a third.

Trade in Stolen Vehicles

In the city of Lubumbashi so many vehicles have right-hand drive that visitors might imagine themselves in an Anglophone country. A rough count made for one hour daily, over a period of one week outside the

Lubumbashi railway station in March 1987, found that about 55% of the vehicles observed had right-hand drive. These vehicles come from Zambia and most of them may be assumed to be stolen. The trade in stolen cars is equally widespread in Likasi and Kolwezi. For the last two years, stolen cars have also been imported from Botswana, because the Zambian government has been cracking down on the thieves, driving them further south to supply their illicit trade.

Several types of theft of vehicles can be distinguished according to the procedures by which it is carried out. Unarmed theft includes: vehicles stolen by means of a counterfeit key, by jumping the ignition, by staged abduction of the driver, and by pre-arrangement with the owner who then claims insurance. Armed theft involves hold-up at gunpoint. To use a counterfeit key, it is necessary to have the co-operation of the driver of the vehicle, or of the mechanic who services it. The key is obtained from one of these persons and a copy made; the vehicle is then stolen while it is parked somewhere. This method is slow but has the advantage that if the thief is arrested by the police the penalty is not very severe.

Straightforward theft through jumping the ignition requires no prior arrangement. The thief breaks into the car owner's premises, forces the car door, jumps the ignition to start the car and drives off. Thereafter he has a key made by a locksmith and repairs the damage. Pre-arranged abduction of the driver is a common practice for stealing trucks loaded with goods. Arrangement is made with the driver to share the proceeds of the sale of the truck and the goods. The driver is then tied up, gagged, beaten and left in the bush. Once the vehicle is safely across the frontier, the Zambian police are alerted by telephone that there is a bound man by the roadside.

When a vehicle is stolen by pre-arrangement with the owner, an agreement is made on the sale price in Zaire of the truck and load, and the owner promises the future thief a percentage of the proceeds. The thief takes the vehicle across the frontier, while the owner declares it stolen to the police and the Zambian insurance agent. After a month, if the police declare that they cannot find the thief, the insurance company pays up. Informants report that this type of theft also is common for motor cars of high value such as Mercedes Benz, BMW, Audi, Jaguar, and Range Rover.

In armed robbery, the vehicle's owner is held up at gunpoint, usually as he leaves or enters his home. This form of theft is the fastest way of obtaining a vehicle, but the thief risks death if he is caught by the police. This form of theft has decreased in Zambia since it became a capital crime. Moreover, international police collaboration has increased. In 1985 several car thieves who fled to Zaire are reported to have been arrested on tips from the Zambian authorities. By 1988 this activity was considered extremely risky.

Obtaining Documents

A number of documents are required to make car ownership legal. The first is an automobile registration card known as a 'Blue Book'. This is obtained for stolen cars at the civic center by various arrangements, each of which has a different price: 500 kwacha gets a new card; 1,000 K gets a card with the stamps backdated for two or three years. A card with all the backdated stamps, the registration number of the car, and the number of its new plate costs 2,500 K. With this last, if the thief is arrested he is covered. The second required document is a sticker showing payment of the road tax. This sticker must be bought each year, and requires presentation of a blue book. The car must in addition have license plates; to obtain these legally a blue book must again be presented. The plates are sold legally in some garages. In 1983 they cost 45 K, in 1984 80 K and in February 1987 225 K. The final requirement is insurance, which varies in cost according to the number of months for which it is issued and the type of coverage. The thief pays an extra sum to get the papers backdated. Once all these documents are acquired, a Zambian driver must take the vehicle across the border; the papers are made out in his name so that it looks as if he is the owner.

At the time of the research, informants stated that it was still possible to obtain the co-operation of the Zambian customs officials, though the price of this co-operation rose continually. In 1983 it was 500 K, in 1984 1,000 K; by 1987 some officials demanded 1,500 or even 2,000 K, to allow a car to pass. If, however, neither the number of the car nor its make, and especially not the name of the owner appeared on the document, then the operation could be repeated several times and payment made with no questions asked.

Earnings

In early 1987, according to informants, a stolen Zambian car in good condition, or even new, could cost from 3,500 to 5,000 K, to which had to be added 2,000 K for the papers, 1,500 K for the driver and 2,000 K for the customs. The buyer made arrangements with the Zairian customs himself. On average, a car in good condition cost 10,000 K in Zambia, the equivalent of 90,000 Z; a car with four-wheel drive could be sold in Lubumbashi for 500,000 to 700,000 Z (62,500 to 87,500 K). This high profit could be obtained by those with sufficient capital and daring at negligible risk.

The men involved in this trade are young, between 25 and 40; they include university graduates. Traffickers say they invest their profits in real-estate from which they earn rent; some are investing in commerce. None mentioned any intention of investing in productive enterprise. Informants at the time of the research, however, thought the trade was diminishing somewhat, owing to Zambia's economic crisis and to increased enforcement of controls and security measures. Fewer vehicles were available, while the number of aspiring traffickers appeared to have increased.

Trade in Stolen Fuel

This trade is in fuel stolen from the mining company in one of Shaba's large copper towns, which, to protect informants, we will call 'Mining Town'. The traffickers are members of the military. They can freely enter the company premises, since they supposedly function as protectors of law and order. The company guards are afraid of them because they are armed. The suppliers are the drivers of heavy machines, trucks and trains. The tanks of some of the heavy mining vehicles hold up to 2,000 l. so the driver can sell two to four barrels of 200 l. in a night. The operation takes place in an unused open-pit mine, where the vehicles are parked. The company guards are seldom there because the minerals remaining on the site have no economic value to the company. If guards should happen along, they share the profits of the sale with the drivers.

The soldiers' wives accompany them, each carrying as many 40 l. containers or 20 l. jerrycans as she can. A soldier buys 20 l. for 50 Z, which adds up to 1,000 Z the barrel. He sells it at the military camp for 1,800 to 2,000 Z the barrel. The civilians who buy the fuel from the soldiers take it to the city and sell it for 2,800 to 3,000 Z the barrel. The company's losses, at a conservative estimate, are at least 500,000 l., or 2,500 barrels of diesel fuel a month.

Fuel is sent in three directions: to Lubumbashi, with transport costs of 1,000 Z the barrel, where it sells for 5,250 to 5,800 Z; to Bukama, a fishing port on the Lualaba river, with transport costs of 500 to 700 Z, where it sells for 6,000 to 8,000 Z, and at peak fishing periods for 10,000 Z; to the agricultural region of Dilolo, Sandoa (see Map 4.1), Kasaji, and Kapanga in western Shaba.[15]

About 70 per cent of the fuel stolen from the company apparently goes to Bukama, where the fishing industry depends on it. During the maize harvest period fuel is sent on by rail to the zone of Nyunzu, in northern Shaba, where a barrel costs 10,000 or even 12,000 Z. It is used not only by truckers but also by cassava/grain mills and electricity-generating plants. The Lubumbashi market is less profitable for this trade because of competition from Zambian fuel of superior quality.

This supply of stolen fuel is crucial to the local economy, not only for the incomes it brings to the military and the drivers who trade in it, but also for the river fishing industry and for the collection of the food grown in the North Shaba triangle around Nyunzu, Kitenge and Kongolo. In other words, the supply of salt fish, maize, cassava and peanuts for the urban markets of the Shaba copperbelt and the Kasai diamond fields depends on this fuel. The trade in stolen fuel also helps to hold down food prices paid by urban consumers. Prices would be much higher without this illegal supply because fuel from legal sources is in such short supply that less food could be collected and urban food prices would rise because of scarcity.

Poaching

To investigate poaching, Dr Rukarangira went by train from Lubumbashi to Luena. There he learned that the best hunting areas were in the collectivity of Butumba 75 km. distant. Military vehicles do not go there because there are no roads, so poachers operate openly. Pick-up trucks can travel the first 35 km. but none were making the trip at the time of the research. The last 40 km. of the journey to the park border is along a narrow path. To get there, he rented a bicycle for 400 zaires a day, riding pillion behind the owner and sometimes taking a turn at pedalling.

The game parks of Kundelungu and Upemba are the areas in which poaching occurs in Shaba. The inhabitants of these parks have always hunted for food, but international trade created the demand for ivory in the nineteenth century. To this, twentieth-century fashion has added demand for hair from elephant tails for bracelets, and for zebra, crocodile and leopard skins. Large-scale international traders encourage African poaching: the lure of easy profits from the relatively high prices they pay propels the local inhabitants to supply animals. Since independence, expansion of population in urban centers has given rise to increased demand for smoked elephant, buffalo and antelope meat, viands of choice for festive meals.

Poaching is facilitated by the ease of obtaining firearms and ammunition, by apparent complicity between some park rangers and the poachers, and by the reported immunity of the big buyers from prosecution because they enjoy political protection. Many hunters use Mauser 52s obtained from the military barracks, for which ammunition is in plentiful supply and difficult to control. A gun costs from 8,000 to 10,000 Z, cartridges from 20 to 40 Z each. In the zone of Butumba where the ivory is poached, 75 km. from Luena (see Map 4.1), which is 400 km. from Lubumbashi, it cost 350 to 450 Z a kg. in March 1987; in Lubumbashi it could be sold for 1,000 to 1,600 Z a kg. The journey from Butumba to Luena is best made at night, preferably by car. The stage from Luena to Lubumbashi can be travelled by truck without much problem, although it is necessary to make payments in order to pass the many control posts. From Luena to the hunting grounds, the journey is by bicycle, as described earlier.

Ivory

Various criteria affect the price of ivory in Lubumbashi. They are: the weight of the tusk (those over 15 kg. have a special price); the color (white is preferable); the depth of the fissures (they vary according to the age and sex of the animal); whether the tusks come from the same animal or not (a pair sells for a higher price than two single tusks).

Ivory bought in Lubumbashi is illegally exported in various directions, according to the orders from the buyer's customers and the location of his trade network. Ivory may go by plane to Kinshasa, and from thence to Brussels or Hong Kong; by truck via Kasumbalesa to Lusaka or to Johannesburg, then by plane to Hong Kong; or it may go to Kalemie on the shore of Lake Tanganyika and then by boat via Kalundu and Uvira to Bujumbura (see Map 4.1). Here it is bought for up to $50 a kg. by traders from West Africa.

There are three categories of traffickers. In the interior, white store-owners buy ivory with the money from their commerce. They take it by truck to Lubumbashi, then send it to South Africa, using some of the foreign exchange they earn to buy consumer goods for their trade and investing the rest abroad. Wealthy Zairian store owners or food whole-salers are also ivory traffickers; they organize their trade by preference through Europeans or West Africans. Small-scale traffickers buy from hunters and go to Lubumbashi to sell; sometimes it is more profitable for them to exchange tusks for ammunition directly.

The floating of the zaire in 1983 stimulated the big exporter buyers because although after passage of this reform the dollar cost more, the purchase price of ivory did not change. Then 1984–85 brought a sharp decline in the trade following the International Conference for the Protection of Nature and the ban on ivory sales in Europe. This was strictly enforced and many tons of ivory were seized. However, 1986 saw the recovery of the market as the trade to Hong-Kong opened up.

The greatest beneficiaries of this trade are the big exporters, most of them foreigners who do not reinvest their profits in Zaire. But some rural inhabitants also benefit. As in former times a hunter must give a tusk to the chief for every elephant he kills. In the villages, earnings from ivory poaching enable chiefs and successful hunters to own houses built of permanent materials. For a village man, gun ownership is thus a sure means of obtaining plentiful food and good housing. Hunting is much more profitable than farming in these remote areas, and growing the family's supply of food staples is relegated to women. Meat is plentiful for those living in the neighborhood of the parks; some is consumed locally, but most is sold.

Before setting off, the hunter engages four to five assistants to help him cut up the animals he kills, and to smoke and carry the meat. He buys provisions for the whole team and bags of salt (imported from the south) for salting elephant meat before it is dried over a fire. Not all hunters are local men. The high price of game meat in urban areas has given rise to a group of traffickers specializing in a profitable trade in smoked and dried game meat. They are as destructive to Zaire's game parks as are the ivory poachers, and use the same methods. They come from Lubumbashi and from East and West Kasai with 52 or 12-calibre Mausers, and seek out a hunter at Luena or Lubudi with whom they contract for the game. As soon as an animal is killed, the meat is divided between them and the trafficker can then buy the hunter's share to add to his own. If the bag is an elephant, the hunter has the tusks, the trafficker the meat. Once the meat is dried and packaged, he takes it to Luena; from thence he sends it on by train. Some of this meat goes to Lubumbashi, but most goes to the diamond-mining center of Mbuji-Mayi in East Kasai where prices are higher.

Traders' Tales

The personal narratives to which we now turn are of interest because they reveal linkages between macrolevel political economic processes and microlevel decisions made by people struggling to survive and to achieve satisfactions in their daily lives. This section presents thumbnail sketches of three traders, two men and one woman, who are active in the cross-border trade in southeastern Shaba.

The first trader, *Citoyen* Kasuku, collects maize in the North Shaba triangle around Kongolo. In this area a ten-year USAID maize production and marketing project constructed roads, bridges and storage points to help traders to evacuate the harvest from villages to the railway, whence it is shipped to mills in the copperbelt. Kasuku began by working for his brother-in-law who owned two trucks. He learned the business and after two years, saved enough to make a down payment on his first truck. An older man, an unrelated member of his ethnic group, stood guarantor for Kasuku with a milling company which signed him on as a buying agent. In 1987 Kasuku managed five trucks: two belonging to the company, one to his patron and two of his own, the second of which he bought through the mill on hire-purchase. The company supplies Kasuku with cash, sacks and diesel fuel for the campaign. In return, he agrees to sell at a fixed price. Over the years Kasuku has built up a series of clientship networks in North Shaba which facilitate his purchases. Some ask him to bring consumer goods from the south; others prefer cash. When the maize arrives in Lubumbashi, the company deducts its credit advance from the agreed-upon purchase price. Then Kasuku calculates his expenses and divides the remainder of the payment with his patron, without accounting his own labor time.

During the period between maize-collecting campaigns in North Shaba, Kasuku trades in other products around Lubumbashi to keep his own trucks busy. This mainly involves cross-border trade, carrying passengers with their bundles of old clothes and plastic shoes southward, and cooking oil, sugar, maize sacks and so forth on the homeward journey. He calculates his earnings at about thirty per cent over expenses. Neither figure includes his labor time. He supports two families and sends gifts to his parents, so his earnings from the cross-border trade are virtually all spent by the time of the next maize campaign. For this he will again obtain credit from the milling company.

Kasuku's first ('official') wife, who was sixteen when they married, lives in a comfortable house he owns near her brother. She and the second wife (who lives in a smaller rented house) compete in producing children. Kasuku says that each time one gets pregnant, the other follows suit. Each wife had three children in 1987.[16] While some other maize traders also have wives in the North Shaba villages, he does not. Kasuku, who left after only four years of secondary school, is proud of his success as a trader. He drives an expensive-looking car, a right-hand-drive vehicle which he actually obtained quite cheaply. Recognizing the insecurity inherent in these trading activities, he is trying to build up capital to buy another house and to replace his trucks which will not last many years on the rough roads. His activities are mostly legal, except for the bribes he pays to lower his expenses in crossing the border and his exporting from Zambia. He comments on the trading strategy of a childhood friend, a university graduate who could not find work in his profession:

> He wants to get rich too quickly, so he continually fails. You can't get rich at all unless you already have a wealthy and powerful family to back you. But at least you can make a living. You have to go slowly, slowly; to establish your reputation as a reliable fellow. *And* you have to show that you know how to share with your patrons. Trying to go too fast means taking big risks, getting into illegal activities and risking getting shot down. You just can't work without patrons. I've tried to counsel my friend to cultivate his relations and find a backer but he pushes me aside. He is too stubborn, too independent-minded.

The second trader, Mama Harishi, has family on both sides of the border and also journeys on business to Kenya and Malawi. She speaks Swahili and Kinyanja as well as French, English and her own language. Twice married and divorced, she has three children in primary school. A younger brother lives with her. He helps with domestic chores and in her trade, taking charge of the children when she is absent. Harishi buys old clothes in Lubumbashi and in Nairobi to sell in Lusaka. Occasionally she comes upon an opportunity to traffic in precious stones or in amphetamines, as well. In 1982 Harishi wanted to diversify into a legitimate business. She

91

opened a small shop in an up-graded squatter zone outside Lusaka. However, when a brother to whom she had entrusted the running of the shop in her absence made off with the stocks and cash, Harishi abandoned that venture. Instead, she invested in building a house with several rooms that she rents out. She and her younger brother sell beer and soft drinks from the house. She then invested in another plot and began construction of a larger house.

Harishi believes that Lusaka offers a more secure environment than Lubumbashi and that her children, who attend a private school located in the city center, are getting a better education than they could in Lubumbashi. Although the new house is still unfinished, Harishi goes there several nights each week to entertain men friends in privacy, rather than having them stay at the smaller house she occupies with her children. Will she marry again? Harishi says no:

> My first husband, an older man, was a tyrant! First he did not want me to trade. Then he wanted me to show him my accounts and turn over all the money to him, even though he was a businessman himself. And he had other women – another wife, maybe two, and girlfriends. He was always bringing home nasty diseases. So I took my daughters and left him. I did alright for myself until I fell in love with a really gorgeous man. I didn't realize that he was just out for my money. He drank a lot. When I didn't give him what he wanted, he beat me, even when I was pregnant with his child. Finally, I had enough. I can live better, and take better care of my children without a husband.

Harishi conducts her trade with help from officials. An attractive, stylish woman in her thirties, she has powerful friends on both sides of the border, as well as in other countries, who make it possible for her to avoid undue harassment. However, her lifestyle places her in a high-risk category for AIDS which is beginning to strike the ranks of traders based in Shaba and Zambia as well as in Kinshasa (Schoepf et al., in press a).

The third trader, *Citoyen* Imara, has not had Harishi's luck. His story illustrates the environmental uncertainties of trafficking for those who operate without protection.

> In November, 1984, I was on my way home to Lubumbashi with a supply of *bande verte* maize bags when I was arrested at the customs post of Kasumbalesa. My papers were in order and I had cash to make "arrangements", but no matter. The customs officials were backed up by soldiers who had orders to arrest all Zairians, following a series of shooting incidents at the border. My cash and the sacks, worth several thousand dollars, were all confiscated. They threw me in a jail overcrowded with *trafiquants*. You have to see the conditions to believe them! An epidemic of diarrhoeal disease swept through the prison and more men went out feet first than standing. I was very lucky not to have died there!
>
> When I finally got out in January I was fifteen kilograms lighter, and my pockets were empty. In Lubumbashi, my family had had no news of my whereabouts all this time. Not hearing from me over the holidays, my wife

thought I was dead. They were hungry and about to be evicted for non-payment of rent. I was ready to break stones to feed them, so I took a job unloading smuggled petrol drums from a truck. I was so weak at that point that I could barely do the job. Never mind, I am still alive, and so is my family.

His story has a darker side. Several years later we were told that security police had wanted to arrest Imara on suspicion that he belonged to a ring of car thieves operating across the border. Fortunately, he was vouched for by an official who is a member of the same ethnic group and so was left at large.

However, the relative who had lent him capital previously refused to do more than make him a small loan to help him pay his debts. Without start-up capital, Imara continued to take risky, low-paying temporary jobs. His self-respect suffered enormously, as did his reputation in the community. While formerly he was known as a moderately successful businessman, henceforward, his frayed clothes hanging from a thin frame and the need to take on odd jobs marked him as a poor *trafiquant*.

Imara is a university graduate, one of the many who has not found professional employment. We asked him to reflect on policy shifts in relation to his own experience. Has liberalization had an impact on trade? Is he personally better or worse off? What could he tell us about others? Excerpts from his replies follow:

Liberalization? They have had us on (*ils nous ont roulé*) with this measure! What they are saying is really the same old thing: "We don't have jobs for you, but the country is full of riches, so *débrouillez-vous*." But the small traders wonder whether liberalization is a survival measure for the people or a way for the wealthy to become even wealthier than before. Everybody races to make money. They are distracted by impossible dreams of getting rich easily through trade, the way big folk have done.

You asked about agricultural prices. Liberalization has discouraged agriculture because it isn't profitable under present conditions. The roads are destroyed in the interior and remain that way. Traders are scarce while producers are numerous. So the traders arrange among themselves to fix prices. Rather than competing, they divide up the territory and develop relations of clientage with some key men in the villages . . . [17] In the beginning (1983) the peasants bought those big radio-cassette players the traders brought with them. This year they don't have enough money to buy batteries. Anyway many of the radios are broken by now. There isn't enough money to invest in fertilizer for bigger yields or in labor-saving machinery, so production doesn't improve.

'You say that the traders are growing richer while small peasants stay the same because of the market structure . . .'

Traders, yes, but not those little traders who go out to the villages in the rural zones. It's the big traders in the city who are benefiting most. They obtain credit for the buying campaign. They furnish the bags and fuel. These men impose their price and the small traders work on the margin between the peasants and these big men. The peasants have withheld their grain several times, trying to get better prices. At least they tried to, but it's difficult to hold out when you need to sell your produce before it spoils. Maize has to be sold before the rains come. Even before that, because insects and rats start eating it . . .

'Does this mean that liberalization has not changed anything?'

Yes, it has changed things. Before, it was mainly the state which profited from the peasants' work. Now it is the big traders, many of whom are in the political system. When they stole directly out of the state coffers people condemned them for enriching themselves at the expense of the people. Now they can hide behind the market, behind the workings of the law of supply and demand.

The lives of individual traders are full of ups and downs and even some of the larger ones tell hard luck stories that emphasize the environmental uncertainties surrounding both irregular and legitimate trade. While few are as articulate about the broader processes in which they are taking part, each story contains elements that bear out the third informant's perceptions.

Conclusion

The aim of this study was to investigate the organization of the second economy, the way in which it is integrated with the official economy, and the effects of the economic stabilization measures of 1983 on the unrecorded trade. It is evident that unrecorded trade across the frontier results firstly, from the Zambian prohibition on regular trade in products such as maize meal, sugar and cooking oil which are state-subsidized, and, secondly, from insufficient food production in Zaire to satisfy local needs. A series of individuals profit from this trade: the traders themselves, the transporters, certain officials and military personnel on both sides of the frontier. Because taxes are used to fund the subsidies, the Zambian state and society are the losers.

The different forms of trade are specific in their organization, but all are carried out by chains of individuals, each of whom plays a distinct role and is bound to the others by ties of self-interest. Most of the traffickers are petty traders who seek to make a living. They are mainly people with little formal education. However, there are also young men among them who have university education but who are unable to find formal jobs. There are also larger scale *opérateurs économiques* who employ many of these *trafiquants*.

Liberalization measures taken in 1983 do not appear to have made significant changes in the activities studied, nor, according to informants, in other ones. The 'underground' activities are linked in a great variety of ways with the official sector. The big companies, sometimes unwittingly, supply the merchandise for illegal commerce, and are sometimes also buyers of smuggled and stolen goods. Illegal trade is one of the means by which people survive or by which they are able to accumulate capital with which to participate in the official economy. It was beyond the scope of this study to gather precise details of the investment of underground profits; clearly this needs to be a topic for future research. However, available information indicates that when traders obtain money in excess of living expenses and operating capital, they are likely to invest principally in real-estate.

We have not been able to estimate the total value of goods moving unrecorded through irregular trading channels in southeastern Shaba.[18] From all accounts, it is considerable. The activities reported on in this chapter constitute a significant contribution to the food supply of the copperbelt cities, helping to compensate for production shortfalls and to keep prices down. They also allow a plethora of petty traders to make a living. Providing food and hope in the face of continuing economic crisis serves a political function; the trade is a safety valve against urban unrest. It is also a vehicle for capital accumulation; the more wealthy and powerful the individual, the greater the opportunities available.

Notes

1. This chapter is based on research undertaken by the authors from 1981–1985.
2. The much larger-scale activities exporting minerals unofficially from the mining region could not be investigated by means of participant-observation. They are beyond the scope of this study.
3. In order to protect informants no further details can be given about their identity. The researchers wish to express their gratitude to all those who contributed to this study, and who must remain anonymous. If the fieldwork has been successful, it is because of the openness and trust with which informants gave of their knowledge.
4. The authors wish to express their thanks to Dr MacGaffey who translated the initial draft of these sections.
5. The traders' narratives and conclusions are the sole responsibility of Dr Schoepf.
6. Muyayalo found that in 1975 half the residents of a peripheral squatting zone of Lubumbashi cultivated food crops for subsistence and sale. Since then, expanding construction has resulted in land shortages around the city. In 1977–79 many unmarried and divorced women in the inner city sold sexual services to support themselves and dependants.
7. 1 kwacha = 8 zaires in February 1987.
8. By April, because of shortages and increasing demand, the price was 70 K.
9. Only a few examples of these taxes are available. Customs dues on a barrel of fuel are 200 Z (kerosene 100), taxes for the zone 60 Z and for OZAC 40 Z. Sugar is 52 Z/20 kg. to the customs, 10 Z to the zone; cooking oil 48 Z/5 l. and 10Z/5 l. respectively, and maize flour 10 Z/sack to the customs and to the zone, 19 Z to OZAC.
10. B.G. Schoepf, interview with Governor of Shaba, August 1981.
11. B.G. Schoepf, fieldnotes May 1983.
12. B.G. Schoepf, fieldnotes March 1985.
13. B.G. Schoepf, interview with Vice-Governor of Shaba, March 1985.
14. B.G. Schoepf, interviews March 1985; Diane Russell, interviews July 1988.
15. It was not possible to travel this route to find out prices.
16. Rukarangira and Walu agree that many women believe that the more children they have with a man the more he is likely to keep them on. However, men may repudiate women with three or four children when they find expenses mounting.

17. In an earlier interview, this trader explained how land acquisitions by members of the political class served as collateral for loans which were used for other purposes and often not reimbursed (Schoepf, 1985).
18. One team which tried to enumerate trucks entering on twenty roads into Lubumbashi recoiled from observing at night because they considered it too dangerous (Flouriot 1986).

5 The Trade in Food Crops, Manufactured Goods and Mineral Products in the Frontier Zone of Luozi, Lower Zaire
MAKWALA MA MAVAMBU YE BEDA[1]

The rural zone of Luozi borders the Republic of the Congo and is linked by extensive trade to Kinshasa to the south and to the north with Brazzaville, in defiance of the official closure of the frontier. Luozi zone produces food crops for the markets of Kinshasa and is, in turn, supplied with manufactured goods from the city, but the higher prices offered for food across the border in the Republic of the Congo and the availability, and lower prices, of manufactured goods there that are scarce in Luozi provide an attractive competing market.

This chapter investigates the effects of the price liberalization reforms of 1983 on trade across the border and on rural-urban commerce, to see if the reforms have permitted farmers to increase production and marketing and improve their purchasing power and lifestyles and, if not, to identify the major obstacles to such improvement. It documents the kinds of goods traded from Kinshasa and the other towns of Lower Zaire to the villages and markets of Luozi zone and across the border to the Congo, the prices at which they are bought and sold, the costs, revenues and profits of the traders, the problems they encounter, how they organize the trade, and the interventions of the state and its personnel. The chapter concludes with an account of artisanal production and clandestine trade of gold.

Methods, Context and Timetable of Study

The research was carried out from 15 February to 8 May 1987. Since any sort of sample survey is impossible on activities that may be clandestine and illegal, the methods employed for this study were the classical anthropological ones of informal interviewing, participant observation and in-depth study of selected cases. Seven research assistants, who spoke Kimanyanga, the local language, and had a minimum of six years of secondary education, were hired locally for research in the

97

collectivities, together with a supervisor; three more researchers were hired to investigate the transportation of goods. This use of local researchers made it possible in a short space of time to find co-operative respondents and establish the rapport needed to obtain detailed information. Data was collected through questionnaires, interviewing and participant observation, and from price lists, administrative reports and other documentary sources.

The study took place in the zone of Luozi itself, on journeys the researchers made on trucks with the transporters, and in the city of Kinshasa. Research concentrated in nine of the ten collectivities of Luozi zone[2] (see Map 5.1), especially in the strip of Zairian territory along the Zaire-Congo frontier comprising the four collectivities of Kimbanza, Kivunda, Balari and De La Kenge; in the gold-mining areas of the collectivity of Kinkenge; and in the town of Luozi. Research assistants travelled on three different truck routes from Kinshasa to Luozi zone, to investigate the expenses and revenues of passengers, traders, and truckers. These routes were: the western route to Yangala market in Kinkenge collectivity; the central route to the market of Nkundi in Mongo-Luala collectivity; and the northern route past selling points along the road, in the collectivities of Kimbanza, Kivunda and De La Kenge. The truck trips and price surveys in Luozi and Kinshasa were carried out in March; the collectivity studies, with the exception of gold mining in Kinkenge, were finished before the end of April.

Research focused on the different categories of people involved in trade: the traders themselves, the truckers, the villagers, the owners of stores and boutiques, market sellers, gold miners and the local authorities. Those carrying on the trade include first, the transporters, who own or rent trucks and who provide transport for passengers and traders and their goods, between town and countryside, and who, in a few cases, buy agricultural produce and sell manufactured goods themselves. Secondly, there are the unlicensed traders, known as *lutteurs*, (literally, 'fighters' or 'strugglers') who are young men or women between 20 and 40 years old, living in the towns (especially Kinshasa). There are more men than women engaged in this trade, but a significant number are women, either divorced, widowed or living in concubinage; married women are rare. The *lutteurs* go to the rural areas to buy foodstuffs to sell in the city, but they are not operating in the official economy because they pay no license fees or taxes to the state. Thirdly, there are the traffickers, also young men and women principally resident in Kinshasa, who bring manufactured goods to sell in the Congo. In contrast to the *lutteurs*, they do not buy agricultural products. Their primary objective is to sell manufactured goods in the Congo and to accumulate as many CFA francs as possible to exchange for zaires in Kinshasa, where the rate of exchange is highest. Like the *lutteurs*, the traffickers carry on a 'parallel' trade and do not pay any taxes.

98

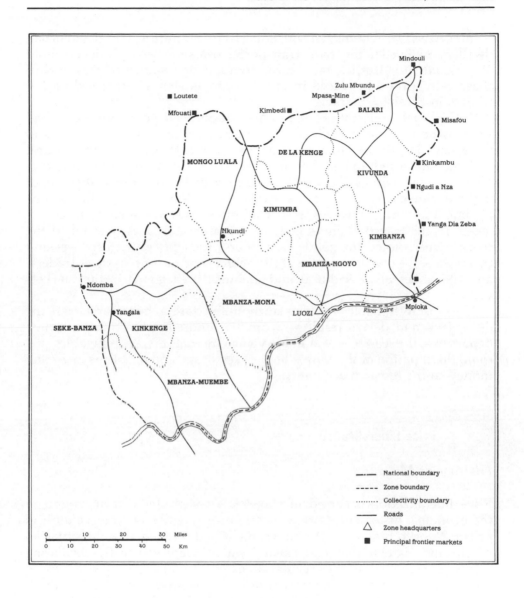

Map 5.1 *Luozi Zone*
(compiled by Makwala ma Mavambu ye Beda)

Interviews were conducted with collectivity authorities, rural and urban dwellers involved in the trade, transporter-truckers, petty producers, gold miners, *lutteurs*, traffickers, and for comparison, women traders in Kinshasa selling food produced in Luozi zone, as well as other sellers and traders in Kinshasa markets.

Within each collectivity, researchers questioned petty producers and store owners in selected villages. Ten rural markets of these collectivities were visited by the research assistants to discover the prices of agricultural and manufactured goods. The frontier areas received special attention because of the number and variety of unrecorded transactions taking place in them. Kinkenge collectivity has extensive gold-mining areas; limitations of time and funds, however, restricted interviews to miners in three villages. In the transport investigation, research assistants questioned the truck owner, noted the goods carried and their price, the expenses and revenues of the owner or renter of the vehicle and of the passenger traders, and the prices of agricultural and manufactured goods in the markets visited.

The most formidable problems surmounted during the research were the difficulties and delays resulting from the unpredictable times of truck departures, the search for a suitable vehicle to rent, market timetables, the rapid depreciation of the zaire which raised costs, and problems in getting money to the research assistants.

Price Liberalization

History of Measures

Price liberalization occurred in stages.[3] It constitutes a turn-around in the economic history of Zaire as it attempts to end state intervention in prices. Prior to June 1981, the government had responded to the situation of chronic scarcity that had existed since independence by regulating prices. Three forms of price regulation existed for agricultural products in the domestic market: the minimum price to the producers, the maximum sale price from the factory, and the maximum wholesale and retail sale prices.

The Executive Council fixed prices and communicated them to the regional authorities, who set local prices either above or at the same level. In reality, however, the authorities were unable to regulate prices, especially during crises, because of the numerous intermediaries operating at all levels in the distribution circuits. Eventually, because of its ineffectiveness, price control had to give way to liberalization.

The decree of 1st June 1981 (*Arreté Départemental* DENI/CAB.018/81) selectively liberalized prices for agricultural products, excluding manioc, maize, rice, cotton, palm oil, sugar and wheat flour. The ambiguity of the measures caused traders to regard minimum prices for these products as ceiling prices. Thus the measure was not successful: it appeared that any sort of price regulation acted to constrain rather than stimulate production and further liberalization was obviously necessary.

The decree of 29th March 1982 (*Arreté Départemental* no. 000110/BCE/Agrirurale/82) abandoned any price regulation for foodstuffs and other products, leaving them to regulation by the laws of supply and demand.

This study seeks to find out if price liberalization motivates producers to increase agricultural production, and if the theory of the reform is, in fact, implemented at the local level.

Awareness and Application of Liberalization

In assessing the effect of the liberalization measures in Luozi zone, the first question is whether those most directly concerned, the local authorities and the agricultural producers, are aware of these measures.

Interviews and questions show that people are, on the whole, unaware of the existence of the liberalization of prices of agricultural products set up in 1981 and expanded in 1983. In general, producers are convinced that the state fixes prices. Some have heard of the measures but say they are not put into effect. Among the local authorities the situation varies; some have heard of the measures, others assert they know nothing about them.

In Kimumba collectivity, for example, the authorities say they have only known about the measures since May 1986: 'We now know that the population can sell their products at any price they like; only over-production can lower prices'. Previously, the prices of agricultural products were fixed by a committee of the collectivity. These same authorities, however, wished to return to the situation of May 1986 and were asking people to hold to previously fixed prices for food crops. In Kimbanza collectivity, price liberalization was only applied to manufactured goods: traders were free to set the prices of their goods but rural producers were not! The annual report of this collectivity states: 'Only the state or businessmen are responsible for controlling prices across the country, so as to avoid inflating the prices of products or goods'. In De La Kenge collectivity, the authorities acknowledged that they had applied the measures at first, but, following abuses in which each individual set his own price for the same product and quantity, they wanted to return to the previous situation in which prices were fixed by a collectivity committee. In Mbanza Mona, a small farmer stated: 'The state keeps an eye on us and delegates the Economic Affairs Service to arrest us as soon as prices don't conform to what the state requires. We are not free to set the prices of our own products'.

In sum, awareness of the measures has not been sufficiently diffused.

Where they are known, they are not always applied, so that price liberalization measures affect only manufactured goods, and not agricultural commodities. Paradoxically, the local authorities firmly believe that by leaving petty producers in ignorance of these measures, they avoid a rise in agricultural prices. Information from all collectivities revealed the same situation: prices were fixed by the local authorities in agreement with the Economic Affairs Service of the zone.

In practice, therefore, the collectivity councils periodically fix the market price of products according to two criteria: devaluation and increases in the prices of manufactured goods. One local official described this arbitrary fixing of prices as 'harmonizing' them! In fact, this adjustment always takes place too long after devaluation or price rises, which explains the continuing extremely low standard of living of the rural population. Table 5.2 gives an example of this practice: it is the literal translation of a circular, one example among many, put out by the collectivity chief in Kinkenge in February 1985, which fixes the prices of agricultural

Table 5.2   Prices of Agricultural Products Fixed by the Popular Committee of Kinkenge Collectivity

FOR GENERAL CIRCULATION

Notice to the Population of the *Groupements** of Kinkenge, Luangu, Luwala, Concerning the Sale of Our Agricultural Products

1. Bottle of oil	10 zaires	Demijohn of oil	140 Z
		Kitadi (smaller local measure)	70 Z
2. Bottle of sugar-cane liquor	3 Z	Demijohn of sugar-cane liquor	30 Z
License fee	4 Z	License fee	40 Z
3. Bottle of palm wine	4 Z	Demijohn of palm wine	40 Z
License fee	5 Z	License fee	50 Z
4. Beans – by the glass×	5 Z		
5. Peanuts – by the glass	4 Z	Sack of peanuts	400 Z
6. Piece of *fufu*** (quartered)	2 Z	Sack of manioc flour	300 Z
7. Rice – by the glass	3 Z	Sack of rice	300 Z
8. Meat – beef		1 kilo of beef	50 Z
9. Meat – game or domestic		1 kilo of game/domestic meat	40 Z
10. Meat – snake		Whole snake	60–70 Z
11. *Nsibizi*† – whole	100 Z	Large *nsibizi*	120 Z
12. Monkey	100 Z	Large monkey	140 Z
13. Chicken – cock or hen	50 Z	Large chicken	60 Z
14. Wild cat	50 Z	Large wild cat	50 Z
15. Manioc pudding	2 Z	Large manioc pudding	5 Z
16. 4 corn cobs – dry or fresh	2 Z	3 large corn cobs	2 Z

N.B. Anyone failing to conform to these prices will pay a large fine to the government.

* administrative divisions
× used as a measure in Zairian markets
** pudding of manioc flour and water
† giant bush rat

products (the original document in KiKongo is reproduced in Appendix 1). The table shows prices for small and large quantities of the listed foodstuffs.

Such circulars provide evidence of the widespread fixing of prices and of the acquiescence of the superior authorities of the zone, sub-region or region in this practice.

Fines for infringement of the prices set are levied by the council of each collectivity. Such sanctions have little effect, however, given the situation of devaluation, escalating prices for manufactured goods, and the attraction of the stronger currency of the Congo; with each devaluation and price increase, petty producers pressure collectivity authorities to increase prices, but usually do not wait for them to do so before charging more than is authorized. But their prices are still lower than they ought to be and thus cannot improve their purchasing power. Table 5.3 shows that the difference between actual prices and those set by the authorities in the collectivity of Kimumba ranges between 33% and 50%.

Table 5.3   Difference between Prices of Agricultural Products Set by the Authorities and Prices Charged in 1987 (in zaires)

Product	Quantity	Imposed Price	Actual Price	Difference	%
Manioc pudding	each	5	10	5	50
Beans	1 glass	5	10	5	50
Pineapple	each	2	5	3	33
Palm oil	bottle	15	20	5	25
Sugar-cane liquor	bottle	5	10	5	50
Vegetables	packet	2	5	3	33
Palm wine	bottle	10	15	5	33
Rice	1 glass	5	8	3	37.5
Manioc tubers	1 sack	250	400	150	37

Source: Archives of Kimumba Collectivity

In conclusion, price liberalization measures for agricultural products are not applied in Luozi zone. Instead the population periodically forces the authorities to readjust the price of foodstuffs to the cost of living. We will show later that the arbitrary fixing of prices is one of the reasons for the trade in foodstuffs to the Congo.

Rural-Urban Commerce: Transporters and Traders on Three Different Routes

Transport trucks travelling the roads of Luozi zone are of two kinds: those whose owners live in the zone and make very irregular trips, difficult to investigate in the short period of the research, and those coming regularly from outside with a timetable of departures from Kinshasa to Luozi zone. In general, the latter co-ordinate with the dates and intervals at which rural markets are held: weekly, fortnightly, or monthly. Three of the many trucks which regularly ply this route were chosen for study. They were selected because their itineraries covered different parts of the zone; information was collected on all of the goods and persons taken on board.

The Western Route

On this route, the round trip between Kinshasa and Yangala market and back (see Map 5.1), *Citoyen* B rented an aged Mercedes 919 truck over ten years old, belonging to *Citoyen* I. Personnel consisted of the driver, a conductor, and two assistants.

On the outward journey, this ancient Mercedes was overloaded with as many as 103 passengers: 74 were men and 29 women; 93 of them were over 20 years of age. The truck also carried the baggage accompanying the passengers, many of whom were *lutteurs* bringing goods to trade, so the truck was heavily loaded. On the return trip, freight dominated the load and there was not room for many passengers. There were only 55, two of whom were simply passengers and 53 were *lutteurs*; all were aged 20 years or over.

Goods and Prices
It was not easy to compile an inventory of the specific goods carried on the truck or their quantity, but it was possible to find out in general the type of goods brought by the two kinds of passengers.

The *lutteurs*, whose purpose for making the trip was to buy food-stuffs from rural producers, loaded up empty boxes for tomatoes and *safous*,[4] and empty sacks for manioc, oranges and avocados for the return trip. Some of them brought with them pharmaceutical products or other merchandise to sell or barter for these foodstuffs. The great majority of *lutteurs* were buying foodstuffs to sell in Kinshasa, but some went to buy gold in the market of Yangala and at Ndomba nearby.

People who were simply passengers had visited members of their family living in Kinshasa and were returning to their villages. They were bringing with them essential items difficult to obtain in the rural areas, such as pharmaceutical products, kerosene, salt fish, clothes, sugar, coffee, tea, storm lanterns, etc.

On the return trip to Kinshasa, goods taken on at Yangala market and along the road consisted of foodstuffs and live animals. Table 5.4 specifies the goods taken on, their purchase price in the rural area and sale price in

Kinshasa, rate of mark-up per unit, and the quantity carried. The total sale value of these products was 317,965 Z, giving a gross profit of 192,810 Z. These figures do not take account of the gold bought by the *lutteurs* for sale in Kinshasa or outside Zaire. Details of this trade and of gold mining will be given later.

Table 5.4 Purchase and Sale Price of Products Loaded at Yangala and Along the Route (in zaires)

Product	Unit	Purchase Price	Sale Price	Mark-Up %	Quantity
Manioc tubers	sack 50 kg.	600	1,500	150	150
Shelled peanuts	sack 25 kg.	375	865	131	1
Oranges	sack	500	1,300	160	11
Avocados	sack 60 kg.	500	1,200	140	10
Fresh tomatoes	box 30 kg.	250	1,000	300	13
Peppers	box 30 kg.	300	1,200	300	9
Avocados	box 35 kg.	250	600	140	7
Bananas	stalk	90	200	122	85
Plantain bananas	stalk	90	200	122	57
Live pigs	–	2,000	4,000	100	1
Live goats	–	800	2,500	213	2
Live chickens	–	100	200	100	2

Foodstuffs are obtained from local producers by purchase or barter. The producers prefer direct exchange of manufactured goods for their products to money, because the latter has little use in an area so ill provided with market stalls and stores. This exchange through barter is also highly beneficial to the *lutteurs*, since they buy manufactured goods cheaply in town and exchange them for foodstuffs which they then sell in town for prices three times higher than their monetary cost would have been in the rural areas. Whether through monetary exchange or barter, this commerce enables a great many people to survive in a situation where jobs are very scarce.

Our investigation in Yangala market shows that the prices of foodstuffs are generally three times cheaper than in Kinshasa, but they are cheaper still if they are bought in the villages along the road. For this reason, *lutteurs* often spend two or three weeks in the rural areas, buying foodstuffs in the villages, bringing them to the nearest market or to the principal road in the region, and taking them by truck to Kinshasa or other towns in Lower Zaire. The purchase price of these foodstuffs is often absurdly low: rural food production principally profits traders and *lutteurs* from the towns, rather than the producers themselves.

Expenses, Revenues and Profits

Details of expenses and revenues of particular individuals make it possible to calculate the profits realized by the different categories of persons involved in this trade.

On the western route, the transporter rented the truck. His aim is to earn as much as he can in as short a time as possible. The trip takes about three days. It is quite usual to overload the truck, as described above, with complete disregard for passenger safety or damage to the vehicle. The transporter's expenses for the trip are as follows:

Rent of truck	36,000 Z	76.4%
Fuel	6,500 Z	13.8%
Oil	375 Z	.7%
Moneys paid to gendarmes	2,100 Z	4.4%
Driver	2,200 Z	4.6%
Food on journey	900 Z	1.9%
Total	47,075 Z	100%

The heaviest expenses are for rent of the truck and fuel. Rent for this vehicle was 12,000 Z a day for three days; 300 liters of diesel fuel were needed for the round trip. An informal tax was paid to the gendarmes at road blocks, consisting of a regular payment at each barrier, amounting to 1,100 Z on the outward journey, 1,000 Z on the return. This was paid in addition to any fines for infraction of road regulations. Although these road blocks are periodically suppressed, they are always set up again after a short respite; their extortions eat into the transporters' revenues.

Revenues from passenger fares and freight charges were 65,000 Z (20,000 Z outgoing, 45,000 Z returning). The passengers do not all pay the same amount of fare. Those who are simply passengers pay more than the *lutteurs*, because the latter are considered to be regular and reliable clients of the transporters. On the Yangala truck, passengers pay 500 Z in each direction; the *lutteurs* only half this amount, 250 Z. There are more passengers going than coming, but more freight on the return trip, and also more traders than passengers. Freight is charged at the following rates: 200 Z per sack, 100 Z per box and 300 Z for a live goat, pig or sheep.

For the round trip Kinshasa-Yangala-Kinshasa, the transporter incurred expenses of 48,075 Z and earned 65,000 Z, which made him a net profit of 16,925 Z in three days. However, more profit can be realized by a transporter who, whether he be renter or owner, follows the example of the *lutteurs* and acquires foodstuffs cheaply through purchase or barter to sell for a high price in Kinshasa. Thus petty trade is often combined with the role of transporter. Since Yangala market is held twice a month, a transporter on this route could bring in 33,850 Z each month, and more if he traded on the side in foodstuffs.

Lutteurs make considerable incomes. A journey into the rural areas by truck carries risks for them, but also opportunities, as illustrated in Table 5.5.

Table 5.5   Expenses, Revenues and Profits of Two *Lutteurs* on the Western Route (in zaires)

	Purchase Goods	Expenses Ticket	Freight Charges	Total Expense	Revenue Sale of Goods	Net Profit
Lutteur A						
46 sacks manioc	22,500	500	9,000	32,000	58,500	26,500
Lutteur B						
2 sacks oranges	1,000	500	2,750		2,600	
20 bunches bananas	1,400				4,000	
4 boxes peppers	1,000				1,000	
5 sacks manioc	3,000				7,000	
Total	6,400			9,650	17,600	8,200

The details of the trade of these two *lutteurs* show that the amount of profit is a function of several factors: the type of foodstuffs bought for sale in Kinshasa, their quantity, and their quality. In both cases, the profits are impressive when compared with the low level of salaries in the city. Since the market takes place twice a month, the two *lutteurs* respectively can earn in a month 53,000 Z and 16,400 Z, from net profits of 45.3% and 46.5%.

The Central Route

The center of Luozi zone consists of the huge valley of the Luala river, an important agricultural area, which extends as far as the Republic of the Congo. Its principal center is Nkundi, which has attracted foreign and national development projects and investments, including a sugar company, Italian economic projects, and COPRA, an agricultural co-operative. Petty producers in this region practice semi-mechanized agriculture of beans, maize, rice, etc. The area attracts transporters, traders, and *lutteurs*, who travel to Nkundi to sell manufactured goods from Kinshasa and to buy agricultural products to sell in the city.

The truck travelled on by the investigator on this route belonged to a transport company working in this area. The driver was himself the owner of the truck; he had two assistants and a conductor. On the outgoing trip, there were 42 passengers, 24 of them women and 18 men. On the return trip, there were 57 in all, with 28 women and 29 men. The number of women on this route results from the economic crisis which forces women, married or single, into trade in their effort to supplement wages and salaries insufficient to feed a family. Trade has become the principal source of income for many Zairians.

The cost of the journey varies according to the distance travelled, the age of the passenger and the nature and weight of the accompanying goods. The adult fare is 500 Z in each direction; children under ten get a reduction of 30% and pay only 350 Z. The fare is the same on the return trip. The *lutteurs*, because they form a steady clientele, also pay a reduced fare of 350 Z in each direction. Goods are charged at the rate of 200 Z a box for manufactured goods, 200–500 Z for a sack of agricultural produce. There are several stages in the journey between Kinshasa and Nkundi, since the truck stops for fuel, for people to eat, and to take on or discharge passengers and goods.

Goods and Prices
The interdependence between town and country is evident in the goods carried on the truck. Besides empty boxes and sacks, the manufactured goods that made up the outgoing load to the rural area consisted of food products, such as flour, salt, sugar, salt fish, canned jam, and non-edible goods, such as cigarettes, soap, etc. Foodstuffs grown in the countryside are loaded for the return trip.

Traders benefit far more than rural producers in this exchange, however, as shown in Tables 5.6 and 5.7, which detail the goods carried, their purchase and sale price, rate of mark-up, and quantity. The sale value of the truckload of goods taken to Nkundi was 243,130 Z, of those taken back to Kinshasa 238,700 Z.

Table 5.6 shows the high prices rural producers pay for manufactured goods, because of mark-ups charged by the traders ranging between 25 and 300%. Table 5.7 gives the low prices these traders pay in Nkundi for agricultural products, which they sell in Kinshasa with a mark-up ranging from 50 to 400%.

Expenses, Revenues and Profits
Ninety per cent of the transporter's expenses are for the truck, only 10% for living expenses, as follows:

108

2 drums of diesel	9,800 Z
Payments to gendarmes	2,000 Z
Truck maintenance	10,000 Z
Food and leisure	2,500 Z
Total	24,300 Z

Revenues from passenger fares amounted to 15,150 Z on the outward journey, 21,900 Z on the return, freight charges to 8,870 Z and 10,650 Z respectively, amounting altogether to a total of 56,570 Z, of which 65.5% came from passenger tickets. After subtracting expenses, the trucker-owner realized a profit of 32,270 Z.

The expenses, revenues and profits of two *lutteurs* on this route are given in Table 5.8. They made net profits of 10,690 Z and 10,240 Z respectively, that is 39.7% and 54.7%.

Table 5.6   Products Loaded in Kinshasa for Sale in Nkundi (in zaires)

Product	Unit	Purchase Price	Sale Price	Mark-up %	Quantity
Salt fish	case	1,850	2,800	51	4
Pilchards (big can)	case	1,560	2,400	54	6
Pilchards (small can)	case	1,200	2,160	80	6
Tomato paste	case	950	1,650	74	5
Salt	sack	300	650	117	5
Flour	50 kg. sack	900	1,500	66	8
Plastic jugs	5 l.	80	200	150	9
Tea and coffee	packet	20	40	100	350
Toilet soap	1 dozen	600	750	25	15
Printed cloth	length	300	500	67	1
Cigarettes	carton	360	500	39	3
Laundry soap	packet	360	540	50	15
Hoes	dozen	2,400	4,200	75	15
Knives	dozen	1,200	2,400	100	3
Machetes	dozen	2,400	4,200	75	3
Margarine	case	1,080	1,920	78	2
Storm lanterns	each	170	350	106	12
Beer – Primus & Skol	case	350	600	71	10
– Castel	case	360	600	67	10
Vicks	each	10	15	50	72
Kinal	pkt of pills	5	10	100	500
Tetracycline	box	2 for 5	1 for 10	300	1500
Nivaquine	box	2 for 5	1 for 10	300	1500
Aspirin	bulk	2 for 5	1 for 5	100	1000

Table 5.7   Products Loaded in Nkundi for Sale in Kinshasa

Product	Unit	Purchase Price	Sale Price*	Mark-up %	Quantity
Beans	50 kg. sack	5,000	7,500	50	20
Manioc puddings	5kilo**	10	30	200	500
Manioc tubers	40 kg. sack	500	1,500	200	20
Gourds	35 kg. sack	800	1,300	63	4
Unshelled peanuts	45 kg. sack	800	1,500	88	7
Peppers	25 kg. sack	500	2,000	300	8
Tomatoes	30 kg. sack	300	1,500	400	6
Plantain bananas	stalk	100	300	200	1

* wholesale price or price sold in truck park
** packed in sacks of 50

Table 5.8   Expenses, Revenues and Profits of Two *Lutteurs* on the Central Route (in zaires)

	Purchase Goods	Expenses Ticket & Food	Freight Charges	Total Expense	Revenue Sale of Goods	Net Profit
Lutteur C						
7 sacks peanuts	4,200	1,210	2,400		11,900	
2 sacks beans	8,400				15,000	
Total	12,600			16,210	26,900	10,690
Lutteur D						
250 manioc puddings	1,250	1,360	2,000		7,500	
4 sacks manioc	1,600				5,200	
5 boxes peppers	2,250				6,000	
Total	5,100			8,460	8,700	10,940

Since Nkundi market is held every two weeks the transporter can make 64,000 Z and the *lutteurs* around 20,000 Z a month.

The Northern Route

The northern route constitutes a great entry-way to the Republic of the Congo. A number of relatively important centers, such as Mindouli and Mpasa-Mine, as well as other frontier markets (see Map 5.1), act as stages between the north of Luozi and the Congo. Proximity to this frontier zone is an advantage for the farmers of the region and for the traders and traffickers of Kinshasa and other urban centers of Lower Zaire.

Several transporters work this route. They have two parking lots reserved for them in Kinshasa. The researcher travelled on a truck that makes a weekly trip, leaving Kinshasa for northern Luozi every Tuesday and returning on Fridays.

Goods and Prices

Vehicles travelling the northern route to Luozi take passengers and merchandise. The persons embarked on the truck we took consisted of personnel (driver, conductor and two assistant drivers) and passengers, *lutteurs* and traffickers. In this case the transporter was the owner of the transport company working the northern route. The truck was a six-ton Renault at least eleven years old!

The truck carried 59 persons on the outward journey; 42 on the return. 51 (86%) of the passengers on the outgoing trip were *lutteurs* or traffickers, while on the return the truck carried the owner, who was moving to Kinshasa, with his furniture and six members of his family, as well as about 36 *lutteurs* and traffickers. Most of those travelling in each direction were aged between 20 and 40 years.

On the outgoing trip the goods carried consisted of food products, such as salt and sardines, and non-food products, such as soap and cement. On the return trip, the *lutteurs* brought back manioc, manioc puddings, and bananas, while the traffickers, having sold their manufactured goods in the Congo, brought back CFA francs to change on the parallel market in Kinshasa.

Expenses, revenues and gross profits of both categories of traders are shown in Tables 5.9 and 5.10. Table 5.9 shows that the manufactured goods the *lutteurs* sell cost much more in the rural areas than in town; gross profits range between 30% and 55%.

Table 5.9 Goods Transported by the *Lutteurs* on the Northern Route (in zaires)

Product	Unit	Quantity	Purchase Price	Sale Price	Gross Profit	%
Soap	packet	3	1,650	2,160	510	30
Cement	50 kg.	2	580	900	320	55
Salt	20 kg.	1	230	350	120	52

The traffickers who sell their goods in the Congo make much larger profits than the *lutteurs*, as shown in Table 5.10. Their trade is more profitable because of the scarcity of particular goods in the Congo and to the very favorable rate of exchange between CFA francs and zaires: in March 1987 it was 330 Z for 1,000 CFA. Trade to the Congo in plastic items, such as mugs, sandals and jugs, has greatly prospered and expanded. This situation presumably results from the lack of any plastic industry in the Congo and the distance of the frontier region from the supply centers of Brazzaville and Pointe Noire.

Expenses, Revenues and Profits

For the transporter, expenses totalled 18,100 Z, primarily for the truck: 12,000 Z for fuel, 800 Z for parking fees, and 2,200 Z miscellaneous; and

111

3,100 Z for food for the personnel. Revenues from tickets, at 800 Z per person and 300 Z each for packages, totalled 139,900 Z, consisting of 92,800 Z for tickets, 47,100 Z for freight. Profits for the transporter thus equalled 121,800 Z.[5] Despite the distance involved, delays at the ferry, and harassment at roadblocks, this commerce holds to its weekly calendar and is profitable.

Table 5.11 gives the details of the trade of a trafficker who has been engaged in this cross-frontier commerce since 1984 and is a familiar figure on the route. This individual is a woman; the *lutteurs* of whom we have so far given details, are all men.

This trafficker rents a vehicle to take her goods as far as Luozi, then travels with them on a truck. She stays two months in the Congo. The income per month she realizes on such a trip is 240,347 Z. Traffickers generally leave from Kinshasa and cross the river at Luozi or Mpioka (see Map 5.1), passing through the small centers of Kintete, Tetelo, Nzale and Yala-Mbundu by truck. Traffickers who then enter the Congo by bush paths, hire porters for an average of 625 Z per porter.[6] These carriers take the goods across the frontier to a stopping place for a truck, by which the traffickers will transport their merchandise to Brazzaville for sale.

Table 5.12 details expenses, revenues and profits for three *lutteurs* trading on the northern route.

Expenditures vary from one *lutteur* to another, according to the type of product and the quantity purchased. These *lutteurs*, like the traffickers, are regulars on this route. They only pay their passage on the outward journey from Kinshasa; on the return journey they pay only the freight charges for their goods. Rates range from 100 Z for a stalk of bananas, to 300 Z for a sack of manioc tubers or puddings.

Revenues are derived from selling in Kinshasa the agricultural products bought in the villages. Manioc is the most profitable commodity. The revenues of *lutteurs* F and G, who sell manioc tubers and puddings, exceed by far those of *lutteur* E, who only acquired a small quantity of manioc puddings and one stalk of bananas. Nevertheless, the profits of the traffickers far exceed those of the *lutteurs*, so one can easily understand the attraction the Zaire/Congo frontier holds for traders. All this intensive and diverse commerce and trade, however, escapes the control of the Zairian authorities.

In conclusion, this trade, carried out by purchase or barter, by which many people in Kinshasa manage to survive unemployment operates at the expense of the rural producers, whose level of subsistence remains extremely low.

Table 5.10   Products Transported by Traffickers for Sale in the Congo

Product	Unit	Quantity	Purchase Price Z	Sale Price in Congo in CFA	in Z	Gross Profit in Z	%
Soap	box	10	3,180	35,000	11,550	8,370	263
Toilet soap	–	24	1,080	6,000	1,980	900	83
Radio cassettes		1	15,000	300,000	99,000	8,400	560
Sacks flour	50 kg.	15	13,500	225,000	74,250	60,750	450
Barbed wire	30 kg. roll	7	16,100	175,000	57,750	41,650	259
Pilchards	box	1	1,440	24,000	7,920	6,480	450
Cans tomatoes	box	12	1,200	10,000	3,300	2,100	175
Penicillin	50 vial boxes	10	12,500	250,000	82,500	70,000	560
TV sets		1	15,000	300,000	99,000	84,000	560
Tetracycline	box	10	13,000	70,000	23,100	10,000	78
Blouses		50	12,500	350,000	115,500	103,000	824
Cheap watches		20	1,200	30,000	9,900	8,700	725
Plastic mugs		50	700	5,000	1,650	950	136
Plastic jugs	10 l.	30	3,900	30,000	9,900	6,000	154
Plastic jugs	5 l.	30	1,950	15,000	4,950	3,000	154
Plastic sandals		100	15,000	100,000	33,000	18,000	120
C.P.A. cloth*	length	5	10,500	62,500	20,625	10,125	96

* manufactured in Kinshasa

Table 5.11   Expenses, Revenues and Profits of a Trafficker to the Congo (in zaires*)

	Expenses	Revenues	Profit
Purchases:			
500 boxes soap	159,000	577,500	
129 sacks rice @ 20 kg.	93,525	170,280	
43 sacks rice @ 50 kg.	77,400	156,090	
Total	329,925		
Transport to Luozi	15,000		
Transport Luozi to Congo	16,250		
Customs	45,000		
Living expenses in Congo			
Rent	2,000		
Other	15,000		
Total	423,175	903,870	480,695

* Exchange rate March 1987: 330 Z = 1,000 CFA

Table 5.12   Expenses, Revenues and Profits of Three *Lutteurs* on the Northern Route (in zaires)

Expenses	*Lutteur* E	*Lutteur* F	*Lutteur* G
Ticket	450	450	450
Purchase of manioc & bananas	700	2,500	5,000
Freight charges	400	1,300	2,500
Total	1,550	4,250	7,950
Revenues			
Sales	1,950	6,700	12,000
Net Profits	400	1,450	5,050

Marketing of Agricultural Products

Luozi zone is a veritable bread basket but lacks any industry. The population is essentially agricultural, employing rudimentary tools and traditional methods which do not produce a large surplus. People primarily grow food crops. Products are sold in the villages, the rural markets, and in Kinshasa. Two big agricultural projects have been set up in the Luala valley, one Italian-Zairian, the other the Kwilu-Ngongo project.

Two kinds of exchange take place. One is the direct sale of agricultural products, the other is their barter for manufactured goods. Rural producers, depending on individual situations, sell their products from their houses, in the village square, in rural markets, along the roads, or, if they are in the border zones, across the frontier to the Congo. Until 1973, they could sell to two Portuguese trading companies, or to Jules Van Lancker (JVL), a large Belgian concern, but since Zairianization, local markets, or traders coming through on trucks, provide the only marketing opportunities. Producers living near the principal roads to the north of the zone or in reach of the Congo frontier thus have a considerable advantage in the availability of alternative markets across the border. In general, however, Luozi zone is disadvantaged because it is far from the main road and rail routes, its roads are in a poor state of repair, and the river crossing is time-consuming. Truckers may own or rent their trucks: out of 19 trucks circulating in the villages surveyed, 13 were rented and six were driven by owners or their employees. In the northern part of the zone there is intense competition and rivalry between Catholics and Protestants.

Rural Markets

A census taken by the Economic Affairs Service in 1980, found 29 rural markets.[7] Our study surveyed ten of them, in eight different collectivities.

Table 5.13 gives the results of this survey. It shows the number of vendors selling agricultural products or manufactured goods, the collectivity of origin of the vendors, and the attendance at these ten markets. It shows the dominance of agricultural products, also that most of the vendors surveyed (86%) sold in their own collectivity. The largest market is that of the agglomeration of Luozi, which is a staging post between the urban centers and the rural hinterland of Luozi.

Table 5.13 Survey of Ten Markets in Luozi Zone

| Collectivity | Market | Number of Vendors | | Collectivity of Vendors | | No. of People at Market |
		Agricultural Products	Manufactured Goods	Own	Other	
Balari	Miyamba†	100	20	n.a.	n.a.	208
Kimumba	Foire**	160	40	148	52	80
Mbanza-Ngoyo	Nkenge-Yengo*	93	12	77	28	186
Luozi and environs	Luozi†	350	95	n.a.	n.a.	2,732
Kivunda	Sundi-Lutete*	59	7	66	0	50
Kivunda	Kinianga*	91	11	100	2	87
Kivunda	Mangembo*	224	33	248	9	316
Kimbanza	Marché du 28**	50	40	75	15	100
Kimbanza	Manianga*	45	20	65	0	180
Mbanza-Mona	Minkamba***	123	18	102	39	89

* held weekly, ** held monthly, *** held fortnightly, †not given

Each rural market is administered by a market office with one to three officials; their role is to maintain security and collect the taxes levied by the Economic Affairs Office of the zone and collectivity. Market taxes vary according to the merchandise and the type of trade practiced. In Luozi zone they consist of the following:

- daily tax: 5 Z
- annual display tax: 200 Z
- daily display tax: 10 Z
- retailer's card: 250 Z
- license: from 640–750 Z
- tax for hygiene service: 250 Z

Marketing of agricultural products is organized according to the weekly, fortnightly, or monthly calendar of rural markets and the arrival of trucks and traders. Forty per cent of markets are held monthly.

Crops get to the market in several stages: after harvesting, they are carried from the fields to the village, usually by family workers; in the village they are packed into sacks and baskets; they then wait for a vehicle for transport to the market where they are sold. Great uncertainty attends

115

the arrival of trucks. The producers often have to throw away produce that rots because the expected truck fails to arrive. For this reason, they prefer the system of filling orders for the *lutteurs*, a practice engaged in by many of these illegal traders.

Unsold Products
Interviews and observation indicate that only about 50% of the food produced in the zone is sent to Zaire's urban centers. Of the remainder, some is consumed locally, the rest rots in the fields or at the roadside waiting in vain for a truck.

There are several reasons why much of the agricultural produce intended for sale never gets to the markets. Many areas are distant from the main roads and markets. Transport is inadequate for getting perishable products, such as oranges, avocados, bananas, pineapples and *safous*, to the market quickly enough after harvesting. Insufficient trucks circulate through the region to collect all the produce available; even though they are large (from six to seven tonnes, loading from 100–120 sacks of manioc), they are quickly filled. Thus farmers who produce large quantities cannot always market them. Traders prefer non-perishable products, such as manioc, beans and peanuts, to reduce their risk of loss. Manioc puddings, which deteriorate quickly in the rainy season, are more usually sold in the dry season.

It is thus easy to understand why so many of the producers near the frontier go to the Congo to sell the crops they produce. Firstly, transport to take their produce to the towns and city is insufficient; secondly, they are disadvantaged by their distance from the principal communication routes.

Some of the food sent to urban centers gets there through the system of gift exchange between people in the rural areas and their kin in towns. Food is sent by the villages to urban relatives, who, in return, send back manufactured goods and processed food. We have no means of quantifying this exchange, but it was possible to make a rough inventory of the commodities sent to relatives in town during 1986, the year previous to the study. The principal towns involved are Kinshasa and Matadi, Boma, Mbanza Ngungu and Lukisi-Kisantu in Lower Zaire. Foodstuffs sent to town consist primarily of manioc tubers and puddings, peanuts and gourds. The most valued products sent by townsfolk to the villages are sugar, salt and salt fish; other goods are cloth and clothing, empty sacks, soap, oil, tomato paste, coffee, tea and beer, pilchards and sardines, flour, kerosene and cooking pots. The cost of transportation is most often paid for in both directions by urban dwellers.

Prices
Producers receive low prices for their crops in comparison to the prices of

116

goods they want to buy, while profit margins realised by *lutteurs*, shown above in Tables 5.4 and 5.7, are high, ranging from 50 to 400%. Prices of agricultural products go up slowly compared with those of manufactured goods. To give some examples, from 1986–87 a 40 kg. sack of manioc tubers increased in price from 350 Z to 500 Z (30%), a sack of shelled peanuts from 900 Z to 1,000 Z (10%), of unshelled peanuts from 400 Z to 600 Z (33%), and of locally-grown rice from 600 Z to 800 Z (25%). The prices of manufactured goods, in contrast, are indexed to each devaluation. Small farmers suffer in these circumstances and cannot improve their conditions of life.

Marketing in Kinshasa

On arrival in Kinshasa, the trucks owned by individuals from Luozi circulate to set down each passenger, trader or *lutteur*. The agricultural products transported to the city are sold from the traders' houses, from the parking lot, or from the market. Sale from houses is organized by the vendors themselves, through loans, payment on account etc. At the parking lot, however, the *lutteurs* consign their goods to sellers (generally women), who come without any money. These sellers come to an arrangement with the *lutteurs* who add 50 to 100 Z per box or sack. After the goods are sold the *lutteurs* collect their money. This system applies particularly to agricultural products sold in bulk, such as manioc tubers, peanuts, *safous*, peppers, tomatoes etc. Goods not in sacks or boxes, such as stalks of bananas and manioc puddings, are sold directly from the parking lot at a price fixed by the *lutteurs*.

The Trade in Manufactured Goods

In the villages, itinerant traders and *lutteurs* arrive with goods and sell them, either directly or indirectly, giving the buyers a few days to find the money. The trader meantime seeks foodstuffs to take to Kinshasa. Sometimes manufactured goods are exchanged in barter for agricultural products. The few rural dwellers who sell manufactured goods also barter in this way: out of 425 sellers questioned in Luozi villages, however, only 8.5% (36) sold manufactured goods, 91% (359) sold agricultural products. In rural markets likewise, 81% sold exclusively agricultural products.

A comparison of retail prices in Kinshasa with those in the villages and rural markets in April 1987 showed a much greater difference in prices of agricultural products than in those for manufactured goods. For manufactured goods, average prices for 152 items in the villages and rural markets, compared with the prices of the same item in the same quantity in Kinshasa, with only six exceptions, showed a difference of less than 50%; pharmaceuticals, being in short supply, showed a bigger difference, from 50 to 70%. The difference in prices of agricultural products in the two areas ranged up to 471% and, in most cases, was over 100% (see Appendix 2 for examples of the latter). But rural dwellers complained of the prices of manufactured goods nevertheless, because the prices they received for the commodities they produced did not bring them sufficient income to buy the goods they needed.

In the survey of rural markets, 48% of the merchandise sold locally by stalls and small shops came from Kinshasa, 20% from Luozi from the branches of wholesalers in Kinshasa and other towns, 16% came from Kimpese. Twenty-one of the store merchants surveyed (58%) used passenger trucks to go to buy their supplies; 6 (16.65%) had their own cars; and others went on foot or by bicycle. They supplied themselves in small quantities, quickly exhausted and continually renewed: 30% of them went to get supplies over 30 times a year, 35% 10 times a year. Expenses were lower for those getting supplies in local towns than they were for a trip to Kinshasa; the prices of the goods bought in the city, however, were lower than for those bought in the towns. For a trip to Mbanza Ngungu and Kimpese, for example, a trader paid 1,490 Z (440 Z for a round trip ticket and 1,050 Z for food and lodging for three days). But a trip to Kinshasa cost 9,940 Z (1,200 Z for a ticket, food and lodging cost 1,740 Z, a taxi-bus in Kinshasa 1,200 Z, and freight charges were 5,800 Z).

The expenses of shop, bar, and kiosk owners in the rural areas also include the taxes they have to pay to the collectivity and zone. In the collectivities of Mbanza Mona and Kivunda, for example, the tax for a store is 500 Z and for beer sales 200 Z, while a license to sell beer is 450 Z. In addition, the zone demands a 500 Z tax from bars and 550 Z for a commercial license. Any bar that plays music has to pay a tax of 520 Z to the sub-region. In addition to paying tàxes and license fees, local merchants are expected to contribute to public events put on by the MPR, such as official welcomes to visiting authorities, including meals, etc. All these expenses reduce profit margins.

The next section is concerned with petty trade to the Congo by small-scale Luozi producers. It addresses several questions. Why do these petty producers sell their crops in the Congo? Which ones do they sell? Who buys them and where? How profitable is this trade?

Trade to the Congo

The Luozi authorities who were interviewed, all stated that officially the frontier is closed, but that they tolerate the current trade across it because they do not know what to do about it. This unrecorded and clandestine trade between Zaire and the Congo is not only typical of the other border regions of Zaire but also of the rest of Africa. Mohsen Toumi describes it as follows:

> In Africa, the circulation of goods and persons continues to escape in large part from the controls and laws of the state. Alongside official exchanges and the network of modern transport, an informal commerce, always more dynamic than the formal, develops in parallel, taking no account of frontiers (Mohsen Toumi 1987: 46).

Frontier trade by traffickers who live in Kinshasa and travel to Luozi and to the Zaire-Congo frontier to sell manufactured goods for high profits in the Republic of the Congo has been described above. In the trade by Luozi producers, the motives most often given for selling agricultural products in the Congo include the following: the unavailability of certain socially-valued goods because of distance from the main supply centers in Zaire; the insufficient number of buyers for agricultural products; the need for more money to pay taxes; ties of kinship and marriage across the frontier; and the devaluation of the zaire and the greater strength and value of the CFA franc.

Means to cross the frontier differ from one collectivity to another. Some people follow the paved roads, as they do for example from Nzala, Mimpela, and Ngobe in Balari. Others use paths, which are sometimes short cuts from the paved roads and sometimes just tracks, in order to avoid the customs posts. Paths are the routes most often followed. Out of 25 people questioned, who sold their goods in the Congo, 22 (88%) travelled on foot, and three (10%) on bicycles.

These small-scale farmers mostly sell agricultural products in the Congo. They include manioc; beans and other vegetables such as peppers, onions and tomatoes; fruit such as pineapples, *safous* and oranges; palm oil; and small livestock. They mostly buy manufactured goods, such as cooking pots, cloth, lamps, basins, machetes, kerosene, batteries, and gunpowder and cartridges, which are hard to obtain in the hinterland of Luozi. They also buy foodstuffs such as salt fish and canned fish, powdered milk, salt, tomato paste, and cooking oil. The recent manufacture of plastic bowls and basins in Zaire has made them a less sought-after commodity in the Congo in this illegal trade; in fact Zairian-made plastic basins are now often sold in the Congo by traffickers from Kinshasa. The exchange of goods in this trade takes place in

119

the frontier villages shown on Map 5.1, and also in Brazzaville and Pointe Noire.

Table 5.14 details the higher prices obtainable for some agricultural products in the Congo, compared to prices paid in the frontier collectivities of Luozi. It is this difference which encourages the producers in the border area to sell their produce in the Congo, in disregard of all official prohibitions.

Table 5.14   Prices of Agricultural Products and Meat in Luozi Zone and in the Congo in April 1987

Product	Unit	Kivunda Z	Congo CFA	Congo Z	Mark-up
Manioc tubers	40 kg.	500	6,750	1,680	3.4
Oranges	1 basket	250	3,800	950	3.8
Beans	15 kg.	350	3,500	870	2.5
Palm oil	20 kg.	400	4,000	1,000	2.5
Bananas	stalk	250*	2,500	620	2.5
Peanuts	45 kg.	800	25,000	6,250	7.8
Pork	35 kg.	1,500	18,000	4,500	3.0
Mutton	30 kg.	1,800	35,000	8,750	4.5
Beef	120 kg.	7,000	120,000	30,000	4.3
Chicken	1.10 kg.	180	1,750	438	2.4
Tomatoes	1 basin	500**	2,750	688	1.4

* price in Balari, ** price in Kimbanza

Gold Mining and Trading

Maps of natural resources show that the frontier zone of Luozi has plentiful deposits of precious minerals, including gold and diamonds.[8] But so far only gold has been mined by artisanal miners in the collectivity of Kinkenge.

Artisanal Mining

The prohibition on artisanal mining discouraged production by this method, but it expanded rapidly after liberalization in 1983. Gold mining started in three villages, Kimwela, Kimbwana and Kinsundi, then spread to over twenty others. The miners mine only gold because they have not yet acquired the technique to mine diamonds. According to the oldest and most experienced miners, there are many indications of the presence of diamonds in the gold fields.

The principal gold miners are the Bayombe, a people indigenous to the Lower River sub-region, bordering on Kinkenge Collectivity. In this sub-region, gold has always been mined clandestinely, which explains the present dominance of the Bayombe among Kinkenge miners. Local Manyanga people from Luozi zone are only gradually becoming involved in this activity; in 1987 65% of miners were still Bayombe.

There are two forms of artisanal gold exploitation: in one, those who have mining rights, or who have acquired them, do the mining themselves; in the other, miners work for those who have such rights. Mining rights are acquired by paying a sum of money to the traditional owner of the land, who then authorizes exploitation of a particular stream and area. In the first form of mining all the gold mined belongs to the miner. In the second, the gold mined is shared equally between the owner or acquirer and the miner. It is appropriate to note here that fraud has already started at the mining site: the miners deceive the owner or acquirer by concealing and keeping for themselves a part of the gold they produce.

More gold is mined in the May to September dry season, when there are no rains, which means there is less water in the pits and mining is easier. On average, a team of six persons working hard can produce between 15 and 30 g. of gold a month. Estimating ten teams per mining village in about twenty villages, the monthly production of gold in Kinkenge collectivity is between 3,000 kg. and 6,000 kg.

Gold Trading

Gold is marketed in various ways. The first is through direct sale at the mining site. The miners do not have access to precise measuring scales, so must construct their own. To make a scale, they use a stick about 8 cm. in length, and two Primus beer bottle tops suspended at each end of the stick by a piece of sewing thread: one of them holds a one *likuta* coin[9] or a match stick as a weight, and the gold is weighed in the other. One *likuta* weighs the equivalent of one gramme of gold.

Gold was sold at the following prices in April 1987:

1 *likuta* = 1 g. = 10 match sticks = 1,400–1,500 Z
1 match stick = 1/10 g. = 140–150 Z
1/2 match stick = 1/20 g. = 70–75 Z
1/3 match stick = 1/30 g. = 46–50 Z
1 *likuta* + 1 match stick = 11 match sticks = 1,540–1,650 Z

Gold buyers at the mining site are called 'trappers'; most of the time they are buying for a third party. They travel on motorcycles provided by the Asians, Lebanese, or West Africans in Kinshasa, Matadi and Boma for whom they make purchases. They buy gold in the goldfields at a higher price than in Kinshasa. They wait patiently and buy progressively as

121

the gold is produced. They may also buy at the markets of Ndomba, Yangala and Zela. No taxes, of course, are paid to the collectivity on these transactions.

Gold bought by these trappers does not pass through the interior Zairian market via the authorized counters. It is smuggled across the frontiers to be sold on the foreign market, where it brings higher profits to the trappers' employers than do legal sales. Some miners market gold themselves; the great majority sell it in Kinshasa, to the licensed counters, to Zairian jewellers, and to foreigners. The latter smuggle it out of the country to exchange for hard currency.

Gold revenues enable those who manage their earnings well to improve substantially their conditions of life. Some miners have improved their houses by buying tin roofs; some have started herds or small livestock-raising projects, or invested in coffee plantations; others have put their money into credit co-operatives or use it for school fees for their children. However, some problems have arisen because of the expansion of gold mining, which may have permanent and harmful effects on the collectivity: schools, agriculture and office work are neglected in favor of mining; prices have risen; malaria, formerly rare, is on the increase; and forests, fruit trees, food crops and springs are being destroyed.

To conclude, although artisanal gold mining has enabled some rural dwellers to earn a reasonable living and improve their standard of living, it is not a controllable source of state revenue, and in addition, it is having some disturbing social, economic and ecological effects.

Conclusion

This study of trade in agricultural and mineral products, and manufactured goods has shown that, in general, the rural producers get little benefit from selling these commodities in local markets. On the contrary, it is the unlicensed traders, or *lutteurs*, who mostly profit from the labor of small-scale producers. An exception however, are the producers who live in the frontier zones, many of whom take foodstuffs to the Congo to sell for higher prices than are obtainable locally. The variation in price between the villages and Kinshasa is greater for agricultural products than for manufactured goods, so that the trade in agricultural products is the most profitable in parallel circuits, either within Zaire or in the Congo. The state receives no revenue from this trade. As for gold, marketing is complex and almost totally escapes state control; much more is sold privately than to the licensed counters. Our study reveals it as a dynamic trade, and again one that profits townsfolk more than country-dwellers.

Notes

1. Translated and edited by Janet MacGaffey.
2. Mbanza-Muembe had to be omitted and only one market in Mongo-Luala was investigated, in each case because of transportation problems.
3. Details are given in 'Evaluation des effets des mesures de la libéralisation des prix agricoles aux producteurs et de réajustement monétaire de Septembre 1983,' *Département de l'Agriculture et du Développement Rural*, Kinshasa, May 1985.
4. A kind of fruit.
5. Payments to gendarmes were not listed for this route (ed).
6. 2,500 CFA. The rate of exchange at the frontier in April 1987 was 1,000 CFA to 250 Z.
7. They are distributed between the collectivities as follows: Balari 3, Mbanza-Ngoyo 4, Mbanza Mona 2, Mbanza-Mvembe 3, De la Kenge 3, Kimbanza 4, Kimumba 2, Kikenge 2, Kivunda 2, Mongo-Luala 4.
8. Présidence de la République, *Atlas Economique du Zaire*, Kinshasa, 1985.
9. The zaire is divided into 100 *makuta* (sing. *likuta*).

6 Women's Trade and Contributions to Household Budgets in Kinshasa[1]
BROOKE GRUNDFEST SCHOEPF & WALU ENGUNDU

Introduction

Throughout Africa many urban women conduct some sort of trading activity. Married or not, employed or not at jobs in the formal sector, they supplement their own or their husbands' contribution to household budgets. This chapter focuses on women traders in Kinshasa to show the role of their enterprises in the upkeep of their households.[2] It details their participation in informal and 'off-the-books' sectors of the economy. Micro-level ethnography shows how people spend money and how much more than the salaries from even relatively high-level professional and managerial positions is needed for a modest standard of living. Women's trade, official and unofficial, is the most widespread source of additional income in these households. Women's life stories are combined with their budgets 'to move beyond the aridity of an unpeopled political economy'[3] and give texture to our understanding of the deepening economic crisis in Zaire. This study is part of on-going collaborative research on women's survival strategies by the authors.

Within the household, gender relations are a critical mediating force between processes of capital accumulation and social reproduction. Gender relations are not static but are continually negotiated. The case studies provide evidence of such negotiation. They also indicate the relative power of women and men and the wider forces they can call upon in their negotiations. Studies of women's survival strategies shed light upon the intersection of social structures and human social agency. They indicate that in most cases, the persistent, courageous action of individuals is insufficient to effect improvement in family circumstances in the face of overwhelming structural constraints (Schoepf 1989 a,b). They also show how gender relations in the household are linked to the reproduction of wider social relations (Schoepf et al. 1990). The analysis is framed to illuminate inter-relations between political economy and culture (Schoepf 1988).

The sample selected for this study is best described as an opportunity

124

sample drawn with three criteria in mind. First, to be included, the women had to exercise some kind of trade. Second, they had to be sufficiently well-known to the interviewer to be willing to provide details of their household circumstances. Third, they had to come from a variety of income, education and social status levels so as to give an idea of existing differences in survival strategies. The relative distribution of wealth and poverty in Kinshasa cannot be determined from this sample; that was not the purpose of the research.

In February to April 1987, Walu Engundu conducted extensive interviews with women and participant-observation of activities in 18 households from different socio-economic levels and zones of the city.[4] In addition, informants were requested to keep detailed lists of expenditures for one month for food and some other items, and in some cases of the sales and receipts of their trading activities. Eight women were wives of skilled workers, semi-professionals or low-level officials; four of middle-level officials or managers in private companies; one was divorced; one was a woman who had a joint business with her husband; two were widows and two were wives of men who had previously been employed but were currently out of work. Three other women were interviewed, but were too often out of town to record daily household expenses. One of the latter was the wife of a high official, while two had unemployed husbands.

The budgets, based on self-report and observation cannot pretend to have recorded all household cash flows, even of the principal female member. However, they indicate an order of magnitude for each household. They show differences in living standards between families at the middle and lower levels of Kinshasa's status ladder. The data complement a large-scale sample survey of household budgets in Kinshasa carried out by Houyoux and colleagues (1986). The data show that:

Recorded expenditures on food and a few other items are extremely high when compared to official salaries. The lifestyles revealed by daily purchases in even the middle management families are not particularly lavish. Most people in many of these households do not get enough to eat, nor is their diet of adequate quality. Incomes and expenditures reported may be compared with the amounts reported by smugglers and traffickers in other chapters:

• Women's licensed and unlicensed or illegal trade is crucial for the upkeep of households, which generally include several – even numerous – other dependants in addition to the couples' children.

• Contributions by women are relatively high compared with the contributions of all husbands. This is true not only of those who are poor and unemployed, but of those who are government officials or middle managers in the private sector as well.

• Non-monetized exchanges in foodstuffs, and clientship or reciprocal favors are crucial for ensuring access to goods and for operating and surviving in the informal and irregular sectors of the Zairian economy.

125

• The personal connections and wealth accompanying higher class position confer significant advantages for entering into the more profitable activities of the irregular sector.

• Many men of the study households also find income outside regular employment, but it was not possible to get information on all the means by which they do so. Nor was it possible from interviewing women to discover what proportion of men's total incomes were contributed to these households.

• Success over the long run is highly uncertain for women unable to call upon favors from powerful political patrons or wealthy relatives. Part of that uncertainty comes from the external environment, part from the demands of wider kin, and part is a consequence of women's subordinate position within the household.

The data resulting from the study are presented in three ways. Table 6.1 summarizes the budgets. These are elaborated in the next sections by moving down the columns of the table.[5] They are followed by selections from life history materials which move across the rows of the table, and present the women's experiences over time, often in their own words. Table 6.2 gives some prices of common foods in April 1987, April 1989 and December 1989. A section analyzing gender relations in women's trade is followed by a summary of the longitudinal findings. The conclusions reflect upon the role of gender relations and the informal economic sector in the processes which reproduce contemporary Zairian society.

Incomes and Expenditures

Household 12, 'headed'[6] by a government official who is also a businessman, illustrates the inadequacy of even fairly high-level salaries. In April 1987, his salary was 35,000 zaires a month, but the household spent 46,880 zaires on food alone during the month. The couple are putting not only their own eight children through school, but also nine children of relatives, and paid 117,360 zaires for school fees in the course of the year. One son is being educated abroad, with fees paid by his mother, who regularly changes money on the black market to send to him. Her extensive, unlicensed import trade is one of the means by which they meet all these expenses. Few other households in the sample live at a level comparable to this one. Nevertheless, other examples indicate that expenditures of middle-level managers' and officials' households far exceed salaries (or the husband's contribution to expenses) and are compensated for by substantial earnings of women's trade. These include Households 6, 8, 9 and 10.

Household 9's recorded expenditures of 40,465 zaires, were only for food (21,757 zaires), car and other transport (7,630 zaires), and family assistance (5,280 zaires). The many other needs of this household were met by the 35–100,000 zaires income from the wife's import trade from Nigeria. She was helped by friends and relatives there. She sold from her house, had no license and paid no customs dues.

Household 10 recorded expenditures of 32,560 zaires, solely for food and shoes. The husband contributed only 13,000 zaires; everything else was paid for by the wife's trade in imported jewelry and in Dutch wax (printed fabrics), bought from Kinshasa wholesalers, where personal connections give her an advantage. She paid no taxes and has no license; instead she bribed the authorities.

The 'head' of Household 6, a middle-level professional, had his official salaries from two jobs, which in April 1987 totaled 6,700 zaires. Recorded expenses of 28,856 zaires for the month, include food, except for fish and meat which the husband bought at reduced price on the job, transport, some clothing and some family assistance. The wife's gross income from selling imported Dutch wax in the same month was 110,000 zaires. Like the wife in Household 10, she makes use of kinship connections with foreign and local wholesalers. Although her recorded business expenses of 3,600 zaires are probably understated, she also has politically well-placed friends to protect her from harassment.

In Household 8, the wife's income from a soft-drink kiosk and bread sales brought in three times as much as her husband's contribution. They provided the family with a calorie-sufficient diet and school fees for six children. Of the other households of lower-paid officials, skilled workers or semi-professionals, the women of Households 1, 2 and 3 made substantial and essential contributions to household maintenance with their commerce, and in two cases with their own salaries, as well.

The widows and wives of the unemployed in the study did not make much income from their trade. They were supported by gifts from kin or by unknown income-producing activities of their husbands. The level of their expenses shows how much income they derived from sources other than their trade. Two women in the sample are widows. One, Household 15, gets gifts from her grown children. Her recorded expenses are for both food and trade. The other widow, Household 16, is supported by gifts from her nephews and her brother (a priest). She recorded expenses of 10,425 zaires over one month for food alone.

Among the unemployed, the husband of Household 17 has two wives, neither of whom were able to make much income from their trade. Yet recorded expenses for this joint household during the month are 6,355 zaires for just food and cooking fuel. Income from the wives' activities supported this family with more cash than many salaried workers earn. Similarly, Household 18 recorded relatively high expenses of 6,696 zaires. These included 4,991 zaires for food, 1,000 zaires for a wife's *likelemba* (a rotating credit association), 530 zaires for a gift and transport for a visiting relative. The husband eats fish or meat on most days, even though he is out of work.

Table 6.1 Summary of Data on Women's Trade, Household Income and Expenditures (in zaires)

Household & Number of Persons	Trade	Licence	Connection to Supplier	Working Capital	Receipts	INCOME				EXPENDITURES			
						Income from Trade	Woman's Salary & Village Gifts or No	Husband's Job & Salary	Husband Contributes	Recorded Expenses	House or Rent/ month	Employees Pay/ month	Children in School Fees/yr.
#1:12 Aloni	Local wax	–	+	16,000	26,000	10,000	+	Mechanic ?	ca. 5,000	9,280	Husb. owns	–	3 / 9,500
#2:8 Mbeya	Children's clothes made on job	–	–	2,000	?	2,458 (estimated)	–	Dispensary supervisor est. 10,000	7,000	15,408	Husb. owns	–	4 / 4,800
#3:10 Tshala	Beer	+	–	4,570	6,450	2,050	+	Party offic. 40,000	13,000	20,941	1,500	1 / 1,000	2 / 1,000
#4:12 Kabamba	Beer	+	+	10,340	?	720	– / +	Bank empl. ?	7,000 (from B-in-L) 1,000	8,205	1,000	–	4 / 7,950
#5:10 Eputo	Makes/sells doughnuts	–	–	7,973	14,055	6,082	– / +	Res. assis. 4,500	2,500	17,963	1,000	–	3 / 300
#6:10 Moseka	Dutch wax	+	+ (kin)	218,000	328,000	110,000	4,700 / –	Res. assis. & teacher 6,700	4,000	28,856	2,000	–	4 / 4,320
#7:13 Gachuka	Wholesale provisions manuf. gds.	–	+ (military)	48,000	?	?	– / +	Army offic. 7,700	7,700 gifts*: 32,780	79,611	Apt. provided to husb.	–	4 / ?
#8:10 Tshungu	Soft drinks & bread	+	–	15,000	28,800	13,000 / 2,800 (bread)	– / –	? 4,901	3,000	11,555	800 Pd. by husband	1 / 1,000	6 / 14,139
#9:18 Mboma	Imp. shoes hsld. gds. wax	–	+	?	35,000 / 100,000	?	– / +	Company mgr. 35,000	35,000	40,465	House prov to husb.	1 / 1,500	5 / 70,000

Household	Trade								Husband			Ownership				
#10:20 Ifulu	Dutch wax	—	+ (kin)	150,000	270,000	120,000	—	—	Gov. off. est. 20,000	13,000	32,560	Husb. owns	—		10	33,000
#11:9 Beleke	Beer	+	—	4,530	?	1,300	2,700	+	Bank mgr. est. 40,000	+	14,987	Husb. owns	1	1,000	4	2,160
#12:17 Kabeya	Beauty salon blouses etc	—	+ (kin)	?	?	?	—	—	Offic. & bus. 35,000	15,000	86,580 ****	Husb. owns	5	10,000	17	117,360
#13:6 Luzolo	Jewelry shirts, wax perfume, etc	—	+	50,000	120,000	70,000	—	+	(divorced) from a physician	17,500 from lover	46,913	2,000 21,000 deposit pd	—		Paid by divorced husband	
#14:10 Rutara	Manuf. gds. food in mkt	—	—	64,170	69,990	5,890 **	—	+	Mkt. seller	—	19,591	1,000	—		2	540
#15:10 Mongongo	Cooks, sells cheap food	—	+	?	11,635	525	—	—	(dead)	gifts from kin	11,110	500	—		4	2,400
#16:11 N'Dongala	Fish & onions	—	+	6,400	?	5,600	—	+	(dead)	13,700 from kin	10,425	Owner: gift of eld. bro.	—		7	1,260
#17:10 Omba Otadi	Cooked fish & meat	—	—	18,410	19,790	1,380	—	+	Unemployed	2,100	6,355	500	—		3	240
#18:18 Tabala	Manioc flour	—	+ (ethnic)	10,000	10,180	180	—	+	Unemployed taxi driv.	?	6,696	500	—		2	160

* gifts made to celebrate husband's promotion but more than balanced by outlays for celebration
** undetermined period
*** household's food taken from trade supplies
**** this household provided food and expenses for about 35 other people during the month

Table 6.2 Kinshasa Prices of Household Consumption Items (in zaires)

Product	Quantity	Apr. 87	Apr. 89	Dec. 89
Cassava meal	50 kg. bag	1,500	9,000	10,000
Cassava meal	2/3 cup	10	50	70
Rice	50 kg. bag	3,000	18,000	19,000
Rice imported	25 kg. bag	1,500	9,000	9,500
	glass (250 g.)	20	150	200
Cassava leaf	big bunch	10	200	250
Amaranthus	big bunch	10	200	250
Palm oil	5 l.	600	1,800	2,000
Palm oil	30 cl.	30	100	150
Salt	*sakombi* (jar)	50	250	300
Salt	glass (350 g.)	30	150	250
Sardines	tin (106 g.)	50	200	250
Soap	brown bar	20	80	90
Ocean fish (frozen)	30 kg.	1,500	18,000	20,000
(Mackerel)	small portion	100	300	500
Beef	1 kg.	500	2,000	2,500
Chicken import. (frozen)	box 14 kg.	5,000	14,500	15,500
Chicken import. (frozen)	1 kg.	500	1,600	1,700
Sugar imported	50 kg. bag	9,850	20,500	22,500
$US1	parallel market	112.5	400	450

Prices of most imported and local foodstuffs rose between 3 and 6 times in the two-year period, while the price of the $US rose 3.5 to 4 times. Some local products, for example vegetables, increased much more. For some products the price increases in bulk quantities were not reflected exactly in increased prices of small amounts. Thus, for example, women who sold rice by the glass in April 1989 made less per 50 kg. bag than they had two years previously.

Most informants did not record outlays for health care. Such expenses for women and children are generally paid by wives, unless the husband works in a private-sector firm which conforms to government regulations requiring employers to provide health services to employees and their first (official) families. Second and subsequent families must provide for themselves.

Wives in Households 5 and 7 recorded health expenditures of 1,900 and 2,490 zaires respectively – about two-fifths of their husbands' official income. Both husbands are government employees and their families have cards which supposedly give them the right to seek care at any health service to be reimbursed by their employer. However, these *cartes d'ayant droit* are seldom accepted outside the government hospital and health centers. Walu comments:

> When a child gets sick and the mother wants to take it to the hospital, she may ask her husband for money. But the latter, especially prior to payday, will say that he doesn't have the money. He tells her to use her savings or housekeeping

money and he will reimburse her. Women complain that husbands seldom repay these outlays. More than one woman has lost her working capital in this way. Furthermore, husbands are not always available. Paying for a child's health care is one of the things that causes women to seek *pneus de rechange* (spare tires), men who can give money in exchange for sex.

Great efforts are made by women, both urban and rural, to keep their children in school (cf Schoepf 1985a *re* rural women). Women make sacrifices in the present to their hopes for the future. The budgets show considerable expenditures on education, mainly from women's earnings. They range from a low of 80 zaires per child per year in a state school in 1986–87 to the 117,360 zaires paid by the wife in Household 12 for 17 children. In 1989 the minimum fee was 6,000 zaires per child. However, it is unlikely that the children of the poor households will progress beyond the primary level.[7]

Capital, Credit and Foreign Currency

Nine of the women in these 18 households started their trade with money given them by their husbands, to which two had added money from a *likelemba,* in amounts ranging from 1,500–100,000 zaires. Four used gifts (50,000 zaires, 4,000 zaires, and two of 50 zaires). Three used savings from their own salaries, ranging from 350–800 zaires. The woman with the highest capital fund, 240,000 zaires, had sold a house in another city. One woman's capital source is unknown.

Rotating credit clubs, *likelemba* and *musiki,* developed in the colonial period to help women get started in trade or meet large expenses (Comhaire-Sylvain, 1968). Women continue to allocate significant portions of their income to this safety net. *Likelemba* funds provide the only form of extra-familial credit available to most women, although one informant reported obtaining a loan from a friend. Few women own property to use as collateral for bank loans.

Those women who imported from overseas acquired their foreign currency on the parallel market. None used the banks, which require importers to deposit an equivalent amount in zaires in a non-interest-bearing account for 3–6 months prior to awarding them foreign exchange – perhaps in insufficient amounts. Many formal sector firms circumvented these regulations in collusion with the bank managers (*Elima* March 22, 1987). US dollars, Belgian and CFA francs are available from money-changers in Kinshasa; some women obtain CFA francs from Brazzaville. Most money-changers seen operating on the street are women. Renowned for their resplendent physiques (*basi ya kilo*), informants affirm that they are protected by men in the political system (Makwala's chapter gives details of the CFA trade). Importers are also said to smuggle gold and diamonds abroad to obtain the hard currency they need to import, and friends of a woman in the study reported that she did this.

Licensing and Premises

Only five women in the study engaged in licensed trade; four of them sold beer or soda and one rented a market stall; such visibility makes it difficult to evade licensing. The other women had no licenses, although six paid to sublet market space. For the most part the women paid no taxes; they evaded the authorities, or customs dues if they imported, by bribing or making 'arrangements' with officials. The middle-class women sold to private clients from their homes, which makes it easier to avoid the authorities. The poor women who sell from stands in their courtyards are constantly required to make small payments to officials who make the rounds of the neighborhood.

Connections and Class Position

To sell profitably from her home, a woman must have connections with a sufficiently large clientele and sell goods of relatively high value, as do the women in Households 1, 9, 10, and 13. These women engage in profitable and large-scale underground trade, for which the connections of their superior social position or their wealth bring an advantage.

The army officer's Household 7, is particularly revealing of the advantages of the personal connections that come with a relatively high position. The husband's official salary was 7,700 zaires a month. The wife has an unlicensed business, on which she pays no taxes. She imports jewelry from Belgium, and foodstuffs from Kivu and Shaba, as well as obtaining supplies of manufactured goods in Kinshasa. Her husband uses his connections to obtain goods and transports them on military and civilian aircraft by private arrangement. The wife buys from 50–100,000 zaires worth of foodstuffs at a time and sells them at wholesale prices to other army wives who retail them.

Social Exchanges

Twelve households receive gifts of food from kin in their village of origin, seven by airplane, one by boat and four by truck. Foodstuffs are also brought by visiting kin, who go home with gifts from the city in return, and often with their fare paid also. Gifts and favors must be reciprocated in some way, even when given in the context of kinship obligations. However, reciprocity is not always weighted or balanced; it may be long-delayed.

Favors resulting from ties of kinship, ethnicity or friendship figure prominently in the trade of the women in the study. They include help in getting supplies through relatives living overseas in Nigeria for Households 9, 12 and 13, through connections with local wholesalers of kinship for Households 6, and 10, friendship for Households 1, 4 and 15, and ethnic ties for Household 18, and free or reduced-cost transport for goods. In Household 16, the son-in-law is a riverboat captain and carries fish without charge. The army officer in Household 7 is also able to ship goods without charge. Other wives of elites were reticent about help received through their husbands' connections.

The more textured data of life histories allow us to understand the complex role played by kin relations in women's trade. The wealthy take on support of elderly or indigent relatives; they house and feed others and pay school fees for relatives' children. Household 12 is putting nine children of relatives, as well as eight of their own, through school. Sometimes family members provide help in the house or in a woman's enterprise in return. Twelve women in the study reported receiving some assistance from family members, including their own children. This help was limited both in quantity and quality. Several women describe their 'disillusionment' with kin, especially junior males, as helpers, reporting that they tend to appropriate goods or receipts. In elite families, schooling and leisure-time activities are likely to absorb much of the young people's time and the return is in 'social capital'.

When families are forced to resort to major assistance from kin, the resulting dependency is experienced as degrading, since there is little of the reciprocity which forms the basis for relations among equals. On the other hand, succoring dependants brings high social esteem and many men collect dependants in excess of their means whom wives are then obliged to find the means to support. Women are more likely to have dependants thrust upon them and are less likely to be able to obtain services or succor in return. Among poor women with very limited capital reserves, family obligations may lead to failure of the trading enterprise. This was the case in Households 1 and 15. While management of resources is conditioned by their availability, households and their members do not make allocation decisions after the manner of managers in a capitalist firm. The life stories presented below indicate that numerous constraints prevent them from doing so.

133

The Labor Day

Too often economists categorize women's trade receipts as 'profit', since without access to other remunerated activities, their labor is, by definition, without opportunity cost. The women in this sample often work long hours and sometimes their labor is strenuous. The labor day includes time spent on unavoidable, time-consuming domestic duties, generally for sizeable families, and time to obtain as well as to sell goods. Four women have salaried employment, as well. Women's work hours vary with class, with the nature of their activity and with the number of salespeople, domestic workers, and children the women can call upon to assist them.

The widow who heads Household 15 walked 8 to 10 km. daily to purchase supplies to make into cooked meals which she sold at noon to workers in the downtown area. Similarly, the wife in Household 5 sets out at 4 am to obtain the ingredients for the *beignets* (doughnuts) she sells to workers walking to their jobs at 6 am. Then, with that money, she repeats her walk to get new ingredients for a second batch to sell to children on their way to school. Later in the day she makes a third batch. The result of this enormous effort is a monthly contribution almost twice that made by her husband, who gave her 2,500 zaires for food and paid 1,000 zaires for rent in April 1987 from his salary of 4,500 zaires.

In sum, the budgets show the high level of household expenditures, compared to contributions from men's salaries or other visible sources of income in all 18 cases. They are an indication of the scale and importance of income generated by women in informal activities. At the least, women's trade provides resources for survival; at the upper end of the scale it provides a comfortable existence for the family. The higher incomes are earned by women in the more lucrative forms of illicit trade which require capital and connections. The study also shows that although high social position and wealth bring advantages in the underground as well as in other economic activities, the obligations of kinship have some redistributive effect. However, the one-month budget records do not indicate the impact of women's trade on long-term family survival. For this we turn to excerpts from women's life stories.

Women Traders' Stories

The narratives presented in this section illuminate the social context of women's trade and household contributions. They help us to understand how gender relations structured in the wider society are reproduced within the family. Following the vicissitudes of these women and their families through time shows the precarious and undependable character of resources derived from the underground economy (also see the chapter by Rukarangira and Schoepf). Gender issues surfaced very rapidly during the course of most of the interviews, as soon as the formal schedule was completed.

Household 1 is fairly typical of a skilled worker's family; the husband is a garage mechanic. In 1987 Mama Aloni[8] was thirty-four. She had five children and the family included three of her female cousins and two nephews of her husband. She does not know the amount of his salary, but he gave her 5,000 zaires for the month of April, at the time equivalent to $42. He also paid school fees amounting to 9,500 zaires in 1986–87. Mama Aloni traded in locally-produced printed cloth which sold well due to a ban on legal importation of Dutch wax.

In April she recorded household expenditures of 9,280 zaires. Her trade brought in 10,000 zaires and she was able to add to her capital. In other months, large expenses for clothing, shoes, medical care and social obligations were subtracted from capital. Expenses were held down by providing only one hot meal per day, with morning and evening snacks of tea and bread.

In March 1989 Mama Aloni travelled to her home village to mourn her father's death. The airfare and contribution to funeral expenses exceeded her capital; gifts from her husband and friends made up the rest. When she returned to Kinshasa there was nothing left to start up her trade again. In any event, local printed cloth no longer fetched such high returns, since the ban on imported wax was lifted and prices of local cloth dropped. To trade in imported wax requires a larger capital fund than Mama Aloni could hope to amass and her clients make such purchases infrequently.

In addition, Mama Aloni reported her dissatisfaction with working so hard to make a comfortable home for the household. She discovered that her husband spent more on his second wife's household than on hers. He justified this breach of norms by saying that she had income from trade to contribute. Mama Aloni protested: 'Why should I work so hard if it doesn't make a better living standard for my children?' However, inflation, the demands of his second family and his own expenses kept *Citoyen* Aloni from contributing sufficient income to maintain this family's modest living standard. In September 1989, the children's morning snack no longer consisted of a roll and milky tea but only sugared water and a small piece of bread.

In Household 2, Mama Mbeya is thirty. She has been married for two years and has not had any children yet. However, the household includes six of the couple's younger siblings, four of whom have been sent from the village to attend school in Kinshasa. Their fees, amounting to 4,800 zaires, are paid by *Citoyen* Mbeya, who also buys clothing for them and some-times for his wife. They live in a small house belonging to the husband situated in a walled courtyard. The house has running water, a shower and a flush toilet.

Citoyen Mbeya is a medical assistant who manages a private clinic owned by a physician. From his earnings he contributes 7,000 zaires per month to the household expenses and obtains free health care for the family. Mama Mbeya works in a tailoring shop where she earns 5,950 per month. In addition, her trade brought in another 2,458 zaires. Thus for the month of April 1987 there were 15,408 zaires for eight people. This household of eight survives with two salaries and Mama Mbeya's extra income.

She began with 800 zaires in capital saved from her salary. She bought some of the dresses made in the shop at wholesale and sold them among her middle-class neighbors and women in her network. By April, Mama Mbeya had accumulated 2,000 zaires which she used to purchase dresses for sale, rather than taking merchandise on credit. By paying cash she boosted her rate of return, which came to nearly 20 per cent that month. Sometimes, when women do not have the full purchase price available, Mama Mbeya sells on credit to be repaid by instalments. However, she is reluctant to do this, because it ties up her small capital fund. Also, she finds that even good friends will 'forget' to pay when they have other payment problems, while neighbors may just move away, leaving her in a hole.

Although a baby would constitute an extra burden just now, Mama Mbeya cannot afford to wait too long. Otherwise her husband's relatives will say that she is sterile and pressure her husband to take another wife. This would be an even greater drain on her financial and emotional resources.

Mama Tshala of Household 3 is a government planner, earning 10,775 zaires in March 1987. Her husband, an administrator in the national political party, contributed 13,000 from a salary which his wife estimated at 40,000. In addition, Mama Tshala made nearly 2,000 zaires by selling beer at a table in her courtyard. Their house, rented at 1,500 per month, has four rooms and an outdoor privy. Mama Tshala's earnings paid for half the expenses of this household which includes eight dependants. She also pays most of the 3,000 in annual school fees for their two children and buys some of their clothing.

As the price of bottled beers[9] rises, illegal home brewing and distilling are reviving. These activities are regaining their place as a source of income for women, especially those women who can use ethnic ties for protection from official harassment (scrutiny). A neighbor of Mama Tshala who for several years carried on a small trade in *lutuku*, a home-distilled alcohol made of maize and manioc, has expanded her operation. Her husband is in politics and she serves several policemen without charge. Therefore, according to Mama Tshala, she does not have to pay fines and bribes which could wipe out both profits and capital of a woman not so well protected.

Mama Tshala's beer business, with a capital of 4,570 zaires, is limited for two reasons. First, she does not see where a wider clientele would come

136

from, since many other women in the vicinity also sell beer. As the crisis deepens and prices rise about three times as fast as government salaries, men are buying less. In April 1987, a bottle of Skol beer sold for 30 zaires equivalent to 25 US cents; by December 1989, the price was 400 zaires, equivalent to 85 US cents on the parallel market. Some customers had stopped drinking except at funerals; others shifted to *lutuku*, which sold at 300 or 350 zaires for a beer bottle-full (750 cl.) or 100 zaires per glass. The second reason is that Mama Tshala is not sure that she would be able to keep control of her beer earnings. Sometimes her husband takes two or three cases to share with friends; sometimes he takes her beer money for himself. Mama Tshala says that when she protests, her husband threatens to stop her from trading altogether.

Citoyen Tshala has a second wife on whom Mama Tshala believes he spends a considerable portion of his earnings, so she feels justified in seeking affection and financial assistance elsewhere. Her lover gave her 10,000 zaires during the month of the budget study, and Mama Tshala is proud to be so highly esteemed. She says the gift made it possible for her 'to join the two ends of the month', but it seems to be more than that. Without a way to invest her capital and savings safely, Mama Tshala will remain insecure for, with her children, her middle-class standard of living depends partly upon a husband and a lover, either of whom could disappear, and a trade from which the returns are dwindling.

Mama Moseka in Household 6 completed four years of post-primary commercial studies. She considers that she is doing very well in her business. Her family is wealthy and well-placed. She reports start-up capital of 240,000 zaires realized from the sale of a house in the interior but does not say how she acquired the house. As noted above she sells imported Dutch wax in the market. Many of her clients are women who bring diamonds from the interior and can afford to pay high prices for the latest *à la mode* patterns. In April 1987 she reported receipts of 328,000 zaires from stock purchased with working capital of 218,000 zaires. She paid 50 zaires per day for the right to place her table in the *Grand Marché* and 20 zaires per day to store a trunk in a nearby house; this last is very risky, as sometimes the person claims the goods have been stolen. Her other regular expense was 1,500 zaires per month for transportation, making a total of 3,600 zaires in visible expenditures. Apparently her profit was 50 per cent that month. Mama Moseka was silent about the 'invisibles', but other traders report that they pay protection in order to avoid thefts by the *balados*, smash-and-grab men who circulate in the market and adjoining downtown streets. The numerous soldiers and civil guard also demand tips. Mama Moseka may give gifts to some of her well-placed protectors.

Citoyen Moseka's combined salaries from two professional jobs yielded 6,900 zaires in April 1987. From this he contributed 4,000 zaires toward household expenses which that month amounted to at least 28,856 zaires (see above). The household includes the couple's five young children and eight other dependents. These are two sons of his elder brother, his younger brother, three of his wife's younger sisters, her sister's daughter and one person whose connection was not noted. School fees amounting to 4,320 zaires for the year were paid by Mama Moseka.

Despite assuming the overwhelming share of household expenses, Mama Moseka says that her husband sometimes badgers her about her trading activities. *Citoyen* Moseka says that his colleagues at work have put him on guard about the sexual misconduct of women traders and he wants to keep his wife from straying. Mama Moseka reports that disputes occur when her husband takes money without telling her what he does with it. While he feels he does not have to justify his expenditures, many women believe that a husband's silence is evidence of his interest in another woman.

> When I refuse to give him money he threatens to stop my trading altogether. When I come home late sometimes from trying to find high-quality wax prints, it also troubles our *ménage*. My husband complains that the housework and child care are sacrificed to my trade. But really, he is nice; his anger doesn't last long. And he helps me with the inventory, he gives me advice and he mostly trusts me.

Citoyen Moseka is aware that his colleagues are jealous of his wife's success and the fact that their household is well-off despite the low salaries paid by their employer. But sometimes, in spite of that knowledge, he falls into the pitfalls these colleagues dig in order to stir up trouble in the family. Walu comments that this is a very common occurrence. Most of his colleagues contribute to their household budget but few have the capital resources which allowed Mama Moseka to launch into one of the more lucrative activities. During the period 1988–89, when the trade in imported wax was forbidden, her influential connections enabled her to keep at it 'from under the table'. The couple is building a house with the profits from Mama Moseka's trade but Walu did not ask in whose name the plot and house are registered.

In Household 7, Mama Gachuka was 35 in 1987. She and her army officer husband have six children and three other dependants. Although trained as a nurse, Mama Gachuka gave up working when she began having children. In 1985 when her youngest was two, she began trading while her husband was posted abroad. Using his salary (4,800 zaires at the time) as capital, she bought chicken, eggs and butter at Nsele, the Presidential estate farm. She disposed of these products among her extensive network of friends and *cousines*: 'With a few telephone calls, in two days everything was sold. I had enough to live on and to buy more produce'. Then she added some jewelry, blouses and novelties imported from Belgium by friends who were airline hostesses. These also sold well.

When her husband returned, he was not at all pleased to find her doing business in his absence. Mama Gachuka thinks he was jealous of her success because his salary was so low. 'He demanded to see my books. But when he saw that everything was in order, he relented.' Actually, her husband now helps her do business. On his trips to the interior he buys local foodstuffs such as beans from Kivu or dried fish from Shaba. He sends them to her on military aircraft or makes 'arrangements' with friends on the national civilian airline, shipping them without charge. Mama Gachuka sells at wholesale prices to other military wives who sell at retail prices. In addition, she sells foam mattresses supplied directly from the factory by a friend at a reduced price. From time to time airline hostesses bring her jewelry from Europe to sell on commission; by-passing customs lowers the price and makes excellent profits. She belongs to a *likelemba* of women traders in which the monthly contribution was 10,000 zaires per person in 1987, equivalent to $80.

At the time her husband's salary was 7,700 zaires, all of which he contributed to the household which, in addition to the couple's six children, also contained three of his young siblings – a total of eleven people. The army provides a car and a driver, an apartment which in 1987 would have rented for 20–30,000 zaires per month, and free utilities. School fees for their children and the husband's siblings are also paid from trading profits. The recorded household expenses of 79,611 zaires in April were unusual, however, for nearly half was spent on food and liquor to celebrate the husband's promotion. The outlay was probably matched by cash gifts from friends and well-wishers, who also brought beer, whisky and food for the fête. Outlays for food, transport, medical care, some clothing, beer, and petrol, as well as two payments of 500 zaires to soldiers as tips for helping out, totalled about 35,000 zaires.

After their initial conflict, which was resolved in favor of her continuing to trade, the couple reached an understanding about money matters. The husband (promoted again in 1989) has a successful career which he uses to facilitate (and participate in) his wife's business as well as to trade himself. She has opened a bank account with his permission. However, they try to keep the capital out of the bank and turning over regularly, since inflation, running at about 100 per cent annually, results in negative real interest. The account is in her name only so that if he should die she and her children would have the money. Otherwise his relatives would take it and Mama Gachuka would be left with only her clothes and jewelry.

They are both contributing funds to build a large house in an elegant neighborhood. The house and land are registered in his name. The eldest daughter is waging a campaign to have her father register the children as owners, so that his relatives cannot take the house from them. This officer is one of the few men in the sample whose wives know what they earn and who turn over their entire salary to their wives. Like *Citoyen* Mboma in Household 10, he can live in the interior on his per diem and other income.

139

Mama Gachuka did not say what her husband's affairs consist of, and apparently he is discreet about them. If her husband continues to rise in rank, more lucrative opportunities will undoubtedly emerge. Mama Gachuka does not believe that her husband has another wife. She is virtually the only one among the married women to express such confidence in her spouse. She knows of mistresses, several of whom actually came to her house when they lived in another city, and casual partners but no socially-recognized wife. Nevertheless, as she observed when recounting the story of a friend who discovered after many years that her husband had a second family with children the same ages as her own, 'A wife is the last person to know'. Her friend was so upset at the years of deception that she wrecked her car and killed herself.

In Household 10, Mama Ifulu is one of the wealthier women in the elite network. She is 44, married, and mother of nine children, all but two of whom are in school. There are also eleven other dependants in the household: five of her young cousins, two sons of her husband's brother, a daughter of her husband's sister, and one unrelated person from her village. The family lives in a large house situated within a walled courtyard. Owned by the husband, the house has electricity, running water and indoor plumbing, and is furnished in European style.

Her husband, who is a middle-level government official, gave her 13,000 zaires for food in April 1987, or just over $100. The household's recorded expenses were 32,560 zaires. There are ten children in school for whom the fees amounted to 33,000 zaires in 1986–87. Mama Ifulu earns the rest of the household expenses by selling Dutch wax prints. She began with capital in goods equivalent to 80,000 zaires of wax print fabrics given to her by her two eldest daughters who travelled to Belgium. Since those first gifts, Mama Ifulu has restocked in the *Grand Marché*, where she knows some of the women traders and is able to get a price well below the retail rate. Her capital has grown to 150,000 zaires in two years and in April she reported gross earnings of 120,000 zaires. Her clients are wives of businessmen and officials. She says that most women in her circle are selling something and doing very well.

Since Mama Ifulu sells from her home, she pays no tax. Her only other expenses are transport of the goods from the market place and, sometimes, clients who take the cloth on credit and fail to repay. When this happens, Mama Ifulu has trouble on her hands, because her husband gets very angry. He blames her for misplaced confidence, not recognizing that unless she extends credit, Mama Ifulu will not make so many sales. He gets even angrier when she uses some of the income from her trade to buy things for herself, especially shoes (more than $100 per pair) and jewelry, without asking him. Walu asked: 'Why don't you ask your husband?' Mama Ifulu replied:

Because he doesn't like me to buy things for myself. He wants everything I earn

140

to go into the house. Then he can give me even less than he does and not lose face. He keeps wanting to know my accounts. He claims he is entitled to 'clear and transparent' management. Why should I have to ask his permission? Whose business is it, anyway?

She did not say whether he has another family, or what income he gets from business he does on the side. Her jewelry is her only property. Sometimes she buys on credit so that her husband cannot take the money she earns, since it is already committed to debt reimbursement, and he would be ashamed if it were known that his wife could not pay her debts.

The recorded expenses were probably an under-estimate for this household of 20 people. Mama Ifulu said she doesn't know her husband's salary. She believes that it is probably somewhere between 50 and 100 per cent more than his contribution to their household and that he has opportunities to make extra money by selling supplies from his job. Her contribution is probably at least twice as much as his. It allows the household to maintain an elite living standard while the husband supports another family and various social expenses which are part of his 'political capital'.

Household 12 lives at a higher standard even than that of Mama Ifulu. Mama Kabeya imports blouses, shoes, and medicines with the help of a brother-in-law who lives in Lagos, and sells them at a stall she rents in the market. She also has a beauty salon, and paid 10,000 zaires in wages that month to five employees. She declined to give details of her finances for fear of compromising her husband, who in addition to his salary, owns a pharmacy and several houses which he rents to foreign businessmen. The family lives in a lavishly-furnished ten-room flat in the city center. The luxury building belongs to the husband. As noted above, the household proper contains 19 people. The husband contributed 15,000 zaires in March 1987 when recorded expenses were 86,580 zaires for the family plus about 35 other people. *Citoyen* Kabeya's father is an important 'traditional' chief, or *Grand Chef coutumier*, and the household was a stopping place for many rural visitors coming to the capital to seek opportunities in school, jobs and trade. All these people ate at the house and many slept there, as well, on mats spread on the living-room floor. As inflationary pressures increased, Mama Kabeya complained to her husband and visitors of her inability to meet everyone's needs. Her husband now rents a small house in a popular quarter for visitors who are obliged to fend for themselves to provide food, transport and health care. This has greatly eased the pressure on Mama Kabeya, who feels that she has plenty to do running her business and managing a large household.

In stark contrast to these elite families is Household 15, headed by a widow, Mama Mongongo, age 43. She has eight children, four of whom are in school. They live in a two-room apartment without electricity; a

141

water tap and a privy are in the courtyard. Mama Mongongo sells cooked food to unskilled workers from government office buildings, policemen and watchmen in the city center. At daybreak she walks 4 km. to the *Grand Marché* or a bit further to the railroad station, to buy produce which she carries home in a basin on her head. She prepares the food on a charcoal burner and then carries it to an empty lot where, arriving just before noon, she lights a fire to keep it hot and waits for customers. Often men take food on credit but fail to pay their debts.

Her rent was 500 zaires per month in 1987; it rose to 2,500 in 1989, and the owner is badgering her to pay a deposit of 22 months' rent. Mama Mongongo is frantic because she does not see any way to raise that sum which in December 1989 was equivalent to $113. Already in 1987 she depended on gifts from kin to meet her recorded monthly expenses of 11,110 zaires, plus 2,400 in school fees for the year. Her receipts from food sales were merely 11,635 zaires, but Walu was unable to determine the amount of Mama Mongongo's capital because she fed her family with the same rice, beans and *fufu* that she sold without keeping separate accounts.

In March 1988, Mama Mongongo was missing from her station in the empty lot, so Walu visited her home to find what had happened. Her sister's child died and she had contributed a considerable sum to funeral expenses, breaking into her capital to meet her family obligations. She didn't have enough money left to start up again and could not find anyone to make her a relatively substantial loan. Walu writes: 'When I went by to speak with her, I found a changed person, very aggressive and at the same time despondent. She no longer wished to reply to my questions'. Mama Mongongo said to her:

> Daughter, ask me for counsel about life and I will tell you, but don't bother me with questions about daily survival! Don't you go to the market? Don't you see how prices rise from day to day? If you don't get any supper, you just stay quietly at home in your place. The rest of us no longer know what to do.

Walu began to give her small sums regularly for, some days, she and her children went without eating. Then Mama Mongongo and her sister obtained a small patch of land adjacent to a military camp. They grow vegetables, sell some and eat the rest. One son has enlisted in the army. Although his pay is very low, when he has been able to make an *opération madeso*, (colloquial expression for 'food gathering operation' or 'beans for the children') collecting tips from passers-by whom he threatens on some pretext, he helps his mother out. Still there is no way she can meet the landlord's demand for advance rent. She has not found a solution to this pressing problem.

The household of Mama Tabala, aged 35 in 1987, also shows how difficult it is for a woman without capital and special skills to make ends meet. When she was 15, she and her husband married in the village; their families

142

were friends. They came to Kinshasa where he was a taxi driver. Their son was born the following year (1968). Mama Tabala has not had another child, but is raising her sister's young son and a niece of her husband. The family lives in a poor quarter in a two-room apartment with a courtyard water tap and no electricity. She cooks outdoors on a charcoal fire. The WC, used by all the courtyard inhabitants, is a hole in the ground without a cement slab.

Citoyen Tabala has been unemployed for several years and drinks when he can find money by working at odd jobs. When he has money he also buys meat and fish for himself. Mama Tabala is obliged to meet all the household expenses by herself. Although her son works from time to time as a mechanic's helper, he keeps the small amounts he earns for his own expenses.

Mama Tabala buys a sack of manioc flour which she sells in small quantities to her neighbors. With that money she buys manioc leaves, palm oil, salt, tomatoes and pili-pili peppers and sometimes a bit of fish. She also has to save enough to re-purchase a new sack of flour. Each month she contributes 1,000 zaires to a *likelemba* and when the kitty comes to her she can buy a blouse or a wax print. Every three months she pays the children's school fees. *Citoyen* Tabala often lies on his mat in the courtyard waiting for food. He eats his meal alone so that he does not have to share the meat or fish with the children or his wife. When Mama Tabala has not sold anything during the day, the children's meal is a porridge of manioc with a little sugar. The neighbors are also very poor and have become less and less willing to feed others' hungry children.

When her nephew fell ill, Mama Tabala used the flour money to pay for a hospital visit and medicines. Then, to buy another bag of flour, she took several sexual partners. Other women in the neighborhood criticized her for this, even though they consider that her husband is very demanding. One, who is more realistic, said:

> Look, you who criticize Mama Tabala, your husbands contribute to the budget, but hers doesn't help at all. There she is, attractive and well-built, still young. She has to feed the family, pay the rent, clothe everyone. What else can she do? If only there were not that terrible new disease that kills, that doesn't let anyone escape.

She took the phrases from Luambo Makiadi's song about AIDS. Actually, the discrepancy between income and expenditures reported in April 1987 suggests that Mama Tabala regularly resorts to casual partners as *pneus de rechange*, to facilitate obtaining goods and to help make ends meet.

Why does Mama Tabala stay married to a man who contributes nothing to family support? Because being married is a more respectable social status than being a *ndumba* (free woman). Nor could she break up her marriage by herself. Her family would have to return the bridewealth given by her husband. This would sour relations with her family and they would not want to do this for such a paltry cause. In their view, other women have to get along somehow (se débrouiller). If she were to return to the village, she would be on her own. Unless she were to find another husband, nobody would help her. So Mama Tabala does the best she can. However, in the presence of a mounting AIDS epidemic, her survival strategy could well turn out to be a death strategy (Schoepf et al. in press; Schoepf 1988). Between 8 and 17% of samples of young women tested in Kinshasa were infected with the HIV-I virus in 1986.[10]

The Mboma household, number 9, has been followed by the authors for fifteen years. In 1987 Mama Mboma was 45, and supplemented her husband's salary by long distance trade. A middle manager for a multinational firm which operates profitably in Zaire behind a hedge of tariff protection from competition with imported goods, Citoyen Mboma was posted to the interior, where he carried on a private trade to support a second wife. His first wife remained in Kinshasa, where their five children were in school. Mama Mboma, the first wife, collected his monthly salary of 35,000 zaires, equivalent at the time to $280. The household included the husband's younger brother, two nephews and niece. The company provided a twelve-room house with a walled garden and a garage, worth about 30,000 zaires monthly.[11] Medical care was also provided. Recorded expenses in April 1987 were 40,465 zaires (see above). School fees and expenses totalled 75,000 zaires for the year.

Mama Mboma made three trips to Nigeria where, with the aid of a relative, she bought household appliances, kitchen utensils, pharmaceuticals and novelties. Her clients in Kinshasa were shop owners and acquaintances who placed orders in advance and paid for goods in instalments. She paid no licensing fees or taxes, but made mutually satisfactory payments (arrangements) to customs officials. While some women trade sex for customs clearance, Mama Mboma is a devout Catholic and considers such practices repugnant. Her working capital of 100,000 zaires brought her 35,000 zaires, 50,000 zaires and 100,000 zaires income, respectively, on three trips.

Returning from her fourth trip, Mama Mboma was cheated by a client who refused to pay for merchandise received. Without a trading license, she has no recourse through the courts. While her other sales covered her travel expenses, Mama Mboma lost all her capital, as well as the profit she had expected to make. Her husband was angry and scornful of her credulity. However, providing goods on credit is the only way to move merchandise rapidly. Rapid turnover is the secret of success in trade, since fashions change so rapidly. When Mama Mboma lost her capital, the household expenses were curtailed: new clothing was foregone; meat, chicken and eggs vanished from the diet. The history of this family illustrates some of the vicissitudes resulting from uncertainties surrounding both informal and formal sector activities.

Gender Issues in Women's Trade

The life histories show the continual process of negotiation of gender relations within the household: gender issues are evident as women describe the constraints on their trading activities. These constraints operate both internally in intra-household relations between men and women, in their relative power and the forces they can call upon in the struggle to control the resources of women's trade. The constraints also operate externally, particularly through the effects of the national economic crisis and the difficulties women face because of gender inequality in the wider society.

The Struggle to Control Trade Resources

Ten of the households studied were getting by in 1987 due to women's contributions to the budget; without these contributions their children and other dependants would have been in abject poverty. However, their capital funds were in constant jeopardy from pressures by husbands and social expenditures including deaths and illness in the family, and these women expressed considerable insecurity. By 1989, four of the ten had failed and one of the six still remaining at a modest living standard operated at a reduced level due to conflicts with her husband for control of her income.

Such intra-household disputes over control of women's incomes and trade resources are common at every level. Several women reported that husbands made serious efforts to learn how much their wives earn from trade, and the uses to which they put their earnings, without reciprocating by sharing information about their own resources. In return, the women went to considerable trouble to cover their tracks and to find ways to create nest-eggs that would serve them in the event of a future reversal in fortunes. The struggle to control resources from women's trade is highlighted by this incident recounted by one informant:

My *cousine* accumulated some capital after her children were grown and wanted to create some security for herself so she bought a plot with an unfinished house. She didn't consult her husband because she knew he would refuse, since he often took her money to spend on other women. When her husband found out about the house, he threatened her: 'Either you give me the deed or I'll throw you out. You can go live in that house and support yourself.'

He brought her father to Kinshasa from the village and told him: 'My wife cannot make decisions without my authorization. Do I know how much she makes from her trade? Perhaps she got the money from adultery?' Her father had received bridewealth which he would have to return if his daughter's husband repudiated her. The son-in-law had always come to his aid when he

145

had a money problem. Besides, he saw how well off his daughter was, living in a big house, with fine clothes, servants, and a car. She should be grateful to her husband, instead of causing problems! He added the weight of his counsel: 'Daughter, he is your husband; he paid bridewealth for you. You are not a kept woman who can make decisions as she pleases. You must follow your husband's wishes. He decides. If he says no, that is the way it is.'

The women in the family viewed the situation differently:

> Women need somewhere to go when husbands replace them with a young wife. Or when husbands die and their families grab everything! Her father was out of his element (*dépaysé*) in the city. He did not see his daughter's contribution to her household, which for some years had been larger than that made by her husband.

Nor did the woman's father apply the old rural norm according to which each person was entitled to the proceeds of her or his labor – a norm upset by the colonial legal system in collusion with male chiefs and judges. He also overlooked the common practice of successful rural women traders, who today build homes in their father's villages so as to have a place to go when widowed or divorced. Conscious of how ephemeral a woman's prosperity can be, the sisters urged the husband to pardon his wife and allow her to keep the house. He refused.

The wife capitulated rather than be held at fault for breaking up her marriage and perhaps even cursed by her father and uncles who would be liable for returning the bridewealth.[12] She ceded the deed to her husband, who sold the house and kept the proceeds. The woman commented:

> Men enjoy seeing women suffer . . . It helps them maintain their superiority to keep women dependent without anywhere to go. If a wife makes 'complications', the man can throw her out into misery. So the wife keeps quiet about his other women, his drinking, his neglect of her children . . . Even if a woman is a successful trader, if she is married, it will be difficult to achieve economic independence and without that, she has no independence at all and must submit to her husband.

Spouses tend to accuse each other of selfishness and favoritism, of attending to personal desires and the needs of their respective families of orientation (parents and siblings) while needs in the joint household go unmet. Women are accused by men of frivolity – using their money for wax and jewelry – and lack of fiscal 'transparency' – covering their tracks. Men are accused by women of irresponsibility; of spending on their own pleasures – drink, tobacco and other women. The majority of informants were aware, and others suspected, that their husbands were supporting (to an unknown extent) the families of other women. Most were angered by this, especially when it was coupled with efforts by husbands to control resources which the informants created by their labor. While the majority had borrowed start-up capital or received it as gifts from husbands, they stated that these debts had been repaid several times over. Seldom was men's right to have a second family contested by wives (but casual sex is contested – especially now, in the presence of AIDS). Wives were more likely to accuse men of dividing their resources unfairly, of favoring the other wife and her family. In the contemporary urban environment, social pressures to obtain a greater measure of responsibility toward women and children than men willingly give, are largely lacking or ineffective. Nor is recourse to the courts an effective substitute.

Women are not well-informed about their husbands' economic activities. Men, however, frequently call wives to account, demanding budgetary 'transparency', while they themselves tend to maintain a code of silence toward their wives about their own affairs, not only about economic matters but about their social lives as well. Such silence is an integral part of their dominance strategy: men's lack of openness allows them to avoid both private and public recriminations, shame and guilt. Sometimes jealous husbands go to great lengths to thwart women's efforts to attain economic security. Women assert that these tactics are used to keep them dependent and subservient while husbands benefit from their labor.

Most women in this sample were married in their mid-teens to older men. But many, even women who marry after completing university education, may be subjected to similar situations and experience similar frustrations (Gould 1978; Schoepf 1978, 1988, 1989 a,b). In view of the fact that so many women share this knowledge, why do they continue to marry? In addition to the pressures described above, informants cited other economic and social factors.

First, although many women are able to make considerable incomes from trade, unless they have special resources such as the education and connections to obtain highly paid jobs, or to obtain special supplies and trading privileges, they will experience difficulty and often great hardship, in supporting a family without some form of sexual dependency and male protection. Second, the status of 'free woman', a colonial category applied to women living outside the juridical control of husbands or fathers, is socially stigmatized (Schoepf 1978). Free women are often considered 'prostitutes'. They may be subjected to all sorts of pressures to supply sexual services to men who are more powerful than they. For these reasons, even for women in professional employment, the status of 'wife', even of second or third wife, socially (if not legally) recognized by payment of bridewealth, may be preferred to the stigmatized status of *ndumba*, an 'empty', no-account free woman. The *vedettes* (star courtesans) of LaFontaine's (1974) study are still in evidence as mistresses (*bureaux*) of powerful men. However, most women seek to transform their status by establishing relationships as junior (and perhaps, preferred) wives.

But women who are married by law or custom are unable to escape from male authority and some successful women traders refuse marriage or provoke divorce, preferring not to see their resources dissipated by husbands with several families. Free to dispose of their sexuality as well as their earnings, they can establish client relations based on the exchange of sex in return for favors. That they do so from a position of power is indicated by the grudging admiration and envy they receive from men and from married women.[13] Wealthy women traders have the reputation of insubordination; for seeking power in relations with men. However, few free women can hope to achieve this status. Many support themselves by selling sexual services to multiple partners, with the attendant high risk of AIDS.[14]

> Complacency about the ability of the urban 'informal sector' to provide people with the means of subsistence is especially pernicious for women and children . . . The vast majority are forced to eke out an insecure existence in petty trade and/or prostitution. The outstanding success of a few women in these occupations should not be allowed to obscure the misery that is the lot of most (Schoepf and Schoepf 1981: 250).

Economic Crisis

The longitudinal data indicate that the deepening national economic crisis and the effects of 'structural adjustment' are creating new difficulties for numerous women who formerly could make ends meet by means of trade. The longitudinal study records the downward movement of the majority of households. The feminization of poverty is evident: women headed households live in dire poverty or insecure dependence on kin and lovers (Schoepf 1988; Schoepf et al.1990).

Of the 18 households in this sample, which is heavily weighted toward elites with higher-than-average incomes, only two were poverty stricken in 1987. In contrast, seven were in serious trouble in 1989. In three destitute households women were the sole source of support. In two households, women took lovers whose gifts meant the difference between dire want and modest sufficiency for their children. Three households, including one elite, had unemployed male 'heads'. One household was in dire straits because the wife of a working class man had used up her capital on social expenditures. This was also the case with one of the widows who was in deep trouble. The other widow scraped by with gifts from kin. Three women turned to gardening: the co-wives of Household 17 descended into a marginal existence in a peri-urban zone, where the women grew cassava in very sandy soil; the widow of Household 15 obtained a more favorable plot through her son.

Gender Inequality in Zaire

Four of the 18 women hold regularly-paid jobs in addition to their trading

148

activities, while all but two (later three) of the men do. Most women are in trade because it is the principal avenue available for generating income to support themselves and their dependants. Only 4% of Zaire's formal sector employees are women.[15] Moreover, while the wages of employed women in the sample ranged between 2,700 and 10,775 zaires per month in April 1987 ($23–$90), salaries for husbands in managerial positions in government and private firms went as high as 40,000 zaires ($333). The scale of opportunities created by employment also varies by gender. In the sample, better-paid husbands tended to have business interests in addition to their formal sector jobs. In several cases their salaried positions provided springboards for more lucrative activities, particularly since wives' incomes were used to maintain households. In this way, women's trade contributes to elite men's capital accumulation and entrepreneurial success.

It is extremely difficult for women without special skills or patronage to find paid employment. Even paid domestic work is a predominantly male occupation. Although sex discrimination in hiring is illegal, many employers express reluctance to hire women because of the high level of male unemployment (variously estimated at 40–60% of urban men). They cite frequent child-bearing with maternity leaves and the heavy burdens of daily domestic duties as factors which make women unattractive as employees unless they have special skills or powerful patrons – or are young and sexually compliant (Schoepf 1978, 1988). Indeed, both poor and middle-class women are burdened by the 'double day' of income-producing and household maintenance activities. However, it is the absence of wage employment opportunities, rather than preference, which relegates poor women to informal sector activities yielding very low returns (Bernard 1972; Schwartz 1972). One result of continuing gender inequality is that, with rare exceptions, women's contributions to household economies do not bring corresponding improvement in women's status in household and community.

Conclusion

This study has documented the substantial contributions of a sample of women in Kinshasa to household budgets. The life stories show how consciousness and social action interpenetrate. Women's monetary contributions to their households are more than just economic acts. They are also a symbolic practice shaped by gendered meanings, constructed and reconstructed in the course of social action. The economic contributions of women and men are related to personal identities in ways as yet unexplored. Wives who work 'for their families' believe this to be a legitimate part of their role even when husbands do not.

149

While gender relations are negotiated, negotiations take place within structures of inequality. Struggles to make a living take place in an environment of scarcity in which differential access to resources, shaped by class, ethnicity and gender, results in extreme contrast in wealth and life chances. The interviews reveal a sharp battle of the sexes occurring in households at all socio-economic levels. Gender conflicts are framed in normative terms. They are mediated by moral discourses elaborated in the process of forging the 'double patriarchy' that resulted from the combined forces of colonial institutions and pseudo-traditions reinvented by the male chiefs and elders collaborating with the 'colonial trinity'[16] of state, church and monopoly firms (Schoepf and Schoepf 1981, 1987; Schoepf 1988). The battle of the sexes appears overdetermined; it is helped along by economics, politics and ideology. Gender discourses, superabundant in the mass media as in daily life, serve to obscure and hence to mute other discourses. Fuelling intra-household struggles, they deflect attention from arenas in which conflict might be more transformative (Schoepf 1984, 1987).

Notes

1. On-going research is funded by grants from the Rockefeller Foundation, Health Sciences Division to Brooke Schoepf. This support is gratefully acknowledged. The authors also wish to extend profound thanks to the women who gave so unstintingly of their time and knowledge despite extremely busy schedules. However, neither informants nor funding institutions are responsible for the authors' presentation of data or conclusions.
2. The term 'household' is used here as a convenient unit for data-gathering rather than as an analytical unit (Guyer 1986: 98).
3. The phrase is from Shula Marks (1987).
4. Households in the sample live in the zones of Lingwala, Kinshasa, Kintambo, Limete, Lemba, M'Binza and Gombe.
5. Table 6.1 and several of the sections which follow were drafted by Janet MacGaffey from Walu Engundu's 1987 research report in French. The analysis was revised and expanded by Brooke Schoepf. The excerpts from women's life stories were written by Schoepf on the basis of discussion with Walu. Schoepf also conducted several interviews in two households in this sample and numerous other life history interviews in Kinshasa and Lubumbashi between 1975 and 1989. The gender analysis and concluding remarks are her sole responsibility.
6. Head of household: *Un seul chef . . .* (cf. Wilson 1982).
7. While 90% of children were reported to be in primary school in 1980, only 20% went on to secondary school and a slim one per cent attended university or technical institutes. The primary and secondary school figures are undoubtedly overstated and offer no information on gender differences. Women made up 7% of university students in 1970 and 14% in 1980 (Walu, interviews for Zaire Country Environmental Profile, 1981). Sixty-two per cent of rural and 32% of urban women are illiterate according to an unpublished study. Moreover, it is unlikely that those who obtain diplomas will find work at aspired levels. Half of those with higher education diplomas were reported to be out of work. In 1984, in the face of population growth estimated at between 2.3 and 3% annually, some 70,000 teachers were made redundant as IMF structural adjustment measures restricted government spending (Schoepf 1985b).
8. Names in this section have been changed to make informants and their ethnic group unrecognizable. For the sake of clarity, wife and husband have been given the same name. This is not the common practice in Zaire among ordinary people, where both partners continue to be known

formally by their own name and women, informally, are called mama of the eldest child. This practice, known as 'teknonomy', used to be applied to men as well, and still is in some rural areas. Among the bourgeoisie, however, wives are commonly addressed as Madame, followed by the husband's name. A few professional women hyphenate their husband's and their own name, as in Europe.

9. Beer is manufactured by Zairian subsidiaries of transnational firms.

10. This sample of women 20 to 29 years includes pregnant women, most of whom were married, and hospital workers, two thirds of whom were single. Neither cohort is as severely endangered as the commercial sex workers mentioned below in note 14.

11. The company may not have paid this much since their lease was an old one.

12. It is widely believed that cursing by elders can bring misfortune or even death to the woman, her sisters and her children.

13. In Kinshasa the widespread Mamy Wata legend is applied to wealthy market women, *basi ya n'zandu*, who it is said, make sacrifices to her on the shore of the Zaire River at Kinsuka. In exchange for protection in obtaining wealth, the mermaid may take a market woman's child or one of her colleagues (Schoepf 1989b).

14. Twenty-seven per cent of a sample of poor women in prostitution were infected in 1985; by mid-1988 seroprevalence had climbed to 40%.

15. This according to a World Bank report cited by Henn, Russell and colleagues (1988).

16. The first felicitous phrase is from Carol Dickerman (1984); the second is from Crawford Young (1965).

7 Conclusion
JANET MACGAFFEY

We stressed at the outset the importance of a new conceptual framework in which to look at the economies of African countries, using the concept of the real, or total, economy, not just the continually diminishing fraction of it that is represented in the national accounts of the official economy. This study of unrecorded trade of the second economy has shown how anthropological methods and insights can contribute to achieving this more realistic approach. It has shown how large and significant a component the second economy is of the real economy of Zaire. Can we conclude, overall, that this second economy is beneficial or not? Our studies show that it certainly has some positive effects; it also has negative ones.

Looking at positive effects first, we have documented how the second economy provides means of survival for much of the population, and enables some people to improve the conditions of their lives. Through unlicensed trade women make up their husband's salaries to a living wage; the proceeds of poaching enable hunters and local chiefs to build better housing; earnings from gold mining and the illegal gold trade have brought wealth to some poor villagers; the proceeds of unrecorded transborder trade are the basis for the operation of flourishing local business, and they generate earnings sufficient to support life in town in Lower Zaire and Shaba.

In some areas, the second economy provides the functioning distribution system so conspicuously lacking in the official economy. In Shaba, Rukarangira and Schoepf show that the fuel stolen from the copper company is crucial for the food supply of the towns: it maintains the fishing industry and riverboat traffic on the Zaire River, and ensures the collection of the harvest in northern Shaba. It thus compensates for the scarcity and unpredictability of official fuel supplies, allowing the food supply to the towns to be maintained and keeping prices lower than they would otherwise be. In effect, this means that the copper company is being forced to subsidize the urban food supply. Theft in this case operates as an unofficial tax to ensure the regular supply of fuel needed for an effective marketing system. In Lower Zaire and Upper Zaire also, unlicensed traders

152

compensate for the deficiencies of the official system and make it possible for farmers to market their crops, by operating in defiance of trade regulations.

Zaire's current political situation and state of economic crisis do not foster the regularity and predictability that Weber finds necessary for economic progress. The second economy is more predictable and rational in many respects than the official one. The data chapters make it clear that illegal and unrecorded trade is not haphazard but institutionalized, operating according to a system of rules known to all participants. Examples include the standardized equivalences observed for barter transactions, the set rates for bribes at unofficial border controls, the arrangements set up for the terms of clientage, and the reciprocal obligations of other personal ties. The personal relationships by which this trade is organized are based on feelings of mutual trust and dependability; they can be counted on in an otherwise unpredictable environment.

The second economy also provides goods and services unavailable in the official economy. It ensures a supply of imports that are scarce through official channels because of the unavailability of foreign exchange. These commodities are obtained through smuggling and barter of export crops, precious minerals and ivory. Of course, if these exports moved through official channels, they would earn foreign exchange, but all too often such earnings find their way into the pockets of corrupt officials. As Nande informants in Kivu put it, 'at least the goods we smuggle are used to import necessities like fuel, vehicles, spares, medicines and building materials, and to keep our stores plentifully supplied with the consumer goods that people want'. The border studies show that goods brought in from East Africa supply stores not only in Kivu but in Bunia in the neighboring region of Ituri too, and that Shaba and Lower Zaire are dependent on smuggled imports. Other sources show that in Mbuji Mayi the stores are abundantly supplied with goods imported with the proceeds of the illegal diamond trade (Biaya 1985: 77). This expansion of local economies in border and mining areas results in some investment of profits earned in illicit trade into legal taxpaying enterprise, which eventually widens the tax base, generates incomes and purchasing power, creates demand for goods, and fosters entrepreneurship. These three studies add some data on such investment to that of my earlier study (MacGaffey 1987), but extensive research on this topic was beyond the scope of this project. Clearly it should be high on the agenda for future research.

Vwakyanakazi has shown how profits from the second economy are used to finance public services that the state has failed to provide, such as provision of health care, construction of a hospital and dispensaries, the building of schools, and road maintenance. Second economy earnings also enable at least some people to pay for these services. He even describes informal tribunals set up for businessmen as an alternative to corrupt local courts.

153

The second economy also provides its own financing. In developing countries, where 80 or 90% of the population has no access to formal financial markets, informal ones provide the sole source of credit and the means for most savings and deposits (Seibel and Marx 1987: 7). Kinshasa's daily newspaper *Elima*, estimated in 1988 that 52% of Zaire's money had circulated outside the banks for at least the last five years, and complained that it was very difficult for Zairians to get credit at the banks. The primary sources of second economy credit for small-scale enterprises are rotating credit organizations. The women Schoepf and Walu studied use these *likelemba* and *musiki* to finance their trade. Another form of second economy financing is found in the loan services popularly known as *Banque Lambert*, but they charge usurious interest rates. Foreign exchange for importing is either obtained by smuggling commodities across the borders or on the parallel money market. More than 1 million US dollars circulate daily in Kinshasa's parallel money market.[1] Foreign exchange can easily be purchased from the 'powerful women' (the *basi ya kilo* of chapter 6) who monopolize this trade. These *dames de bronze* openly trade currencies in certain areas of the city (*Elima* 4 March 1988).[2] Makwala details the trade that supplies some of the CFA francs to this market.

To some extent, therefore, the second economy generates not only alternative economic opportunities for people but even an alternative society, with parallel social and religious institutions alongside official ones.[3] It has, however, some very negative aspects.

Access to the necessary resources to participate in the second economy is extremely uneven and intensely competitive. The rich and powerful, and those who have jobs, have greater access than do the unemployed, the urban poor, and rural producers. Women with high social position or good contacts engage in profitable trade, while the struggle for poor women to support their children intensifies. Thus the gap between rich and poor continually widens. The need to supplement meagre wages at all levels of the work force and bureaucracy through second economy activities means that the state and other employers pay only a small part of the money needed to make up a living wage; the rest is paid by the population at large in the form of unofficial payments or bribes for services or job performance, and in higher prices because goods have passed through the hands of several intermediaries. These extortionate levies which subsidize the wage bill constitute a form of tax but, unlike official taxes, they are not returned to those who pay them in the form of services and infrastructural maintenance. They are levied on second and official economy activities alike: the payoffs to the authorities by those engaged in various forms of illegal trade have been amply documented in these studies.

The smuggled imports that make up for what would otherwise be shortages of some commodities are not evenly distributed throughout the country, but are confined to the regional areas in which unrecorded trade circuits operate. In any case, in the absence of centralized planning, not all essential goods and materials are imported in this way. Smuggling of primary export commodities does supply some regions with needed goods, but it increases the country's shortage of the foreign exchange needed for essential materials for industry and maintenance of the infrastructure. Furthermore, smuggling of food crops out of the country for personal profit compels Zaire to spend scarce foreign exchange on importing food while the infrastructure and industry are neglected.[4] The second economy is in this way depleting the resources of the formal economy in a way that detracts from the rebuilding of the real economy. In North Kivu, Vwakyanakazi has shown that private investment remedies some of the deficiencies of state provision of basic services and road maintenance. This privatization occurs elsewhere also but it is sporadic and cannot compensate for the gross deprivation most regions suffer in this respect. The increasing privatization of education and health care, however, means that it is very expensive. In the cities, the burden of these increased costs falls to a large extent on women, since they are often the principal providers for households.

Labor shortages and disruption of social life are other detrimental effects of the second economy. The rush into artisanal production and smuggling of gold and diamonds has resulted in massive desertions of plantation labor. Teachers and pupils alike desert schools for gold and diamond digging;[5] some women have abandoned their households and the struggle to make ends meet in town, to earn money by selling food or by prostituting themselves in the mining camps, disrupting family life and child care (Tshibanza and Tshimanga 1985: 344–45).

The quality of life for those who participate in the second economy can be very poor. In the mining camps, living and working conditions and health care are appalling. In the cities, as Walu and Schoepf have shown, women struggling to support their families on petty trade are often unable to ensure that their children are adequately fed and cared for. Private and public disregard for safety measures brings injury and death; the overloaded, poorly-maintained trucks that Makwala writes about contribute to Zaire's high rate of serious road accidents.

De Soto points out other ways in which informality involves tremendous costs. Informal businessmen suffer not only from their illegality but also from the absence of a legal system that guarantees their property rights and contracts and helps to promote their economic efficiency. The costs of evading taxes and laws prevent them from using anything but methods low in productivity and technology. Although they save the legal costs of compliance, they must bear the cost of avoiding penalties (De Soto: 153–8). In Peru, De Soto concludes:

> We gradually discovered that informality is not the best of all possible worlds, that it involves tremendous costs, that people try to offset these costs in all

155

kinds of novel but inadequate ways, that lawbreaking is not, on balance, desirable, and that the apparent chaos, waste of resources, invasions, and everyday courage are the informals' desperate and enterprising attempts to build an alternative system to the one that has denied them its protection (ibid: 152).

Were it not for the illicit trade that we have documented here, Zaire's people would be suffering even more acutely for lack of food and needed commodities; it would also be impossible for many rural producers to market their crops. Yet Makwala estimates that nevertheless only about 50% of the crops produced in Luozi are marketed; some is consumed but much food simply rots. The second economy, though operating better than the official one in many respects, still leaves much to be desired.

How then should policy planners and aid organizations approach the phenomenon of the second economy? Policies aimed at improving peoples' lives by removing the severe constraints of inadequate transportation infrastructure, insufficient access to credit, poor communication and information systems, and reducing high transaction costs appear to have the potential to generate very positive results. However, although the World Bank and other aid organizations have expended great effort in some of these areas, political problems and corruption have interfered with implementation, preventing reform of the system and the expected benefits of aid.

Political constraints also limit the expansion of second economy business: the bigger and more visible the enterprise, the more necessary it is that the entrepreneur develop some sort of political accommodation or connections to prevent extortionate taxation or regulation, or outright takeover. It is here that the dynamics of class struggle become apparent. Members of the state-based class attempt to close their class boundary by restricting the socio-economic mobility which others seek by accumulating wealth in second economy activities. But they are not always able to do so effectively: the drastic decline in the administrative capacity of the state since the mid-seventies has reduced its effectiveness as an instrument to serve their interests. On the other hand, the dominant class might come to see that economic stabilization due to the expansion of local business would serve their interests in the long term. It might be possible, as De Soto advocates for Peru, to integrate formal and informal systems by removing unproductive restrictions, incorporating everyone into a new formality, and reforming the legal order to adapt it to new realities (ibid: 240–246).

How people really live in Africa is not reflected in employment and unemployment figures. If policy planners are going to address the problems that ordinary people face, they must move beyond the confines of labor market analysis and instead see the urban economy as providing a range of income-generating opportunities, and investigate what these are and what constrains them.

It is not jobs *per se* but how jobs combine with other key elements in urban subsistence, such as housing, the division of labor within a household and the household's consumption patterns or social networks, that provide different opportunity sets for people in broadly similar economic positions. This often has the effect of leading even the urban poor to see themselves as being confronted by choice as well as constraint in the labor market (Roberts 1988: 11).

Because people take advantage of any available opportunity, we need to look at the full spectrum of institutions that families and individuals use to satisfy their needs, either in the formal economy or outside it (Witte 1987: 78). This recommendation has wide relevance within Africa, since the situation we have described is not particular to Zaire but is widespread throughout the continent.

The Zairian state furthers the interests of the state-based class by repressing the population and providing access to lucrative opportunities in the second economy for those holding state position. We have said that participation in the second economy can be seen as a political option: by contesting what is defined as legitimate, people confront a predatory state which fails to provide them with the opportunity to earn a living wage, with a functioning economic infrastructure or with basic social services. In refusing to comply with regulations and restrictions, they are expressing resistance to the state and to the class which controls it. A similar assessment is made in Tanzania:

> Second economy activities are not a political threat, at least not at present, but they certainly pose an economic challenge to the official establishment. State legitimacy is threatened in the sense that the challenge to the official economy makes official policies and distributive channels ineffective by diverting the flow of goods and services and by creating its own rent levels (Maliyamkono and Bagachwa 1990: 134).

States such as Zaire are described as mercantilist, meaning states in which the economy is governed by politics not by markets, and where entry to the market is restricted not free. De Soto says of Peru: 'The *raison d'être* of the mercantilist state was to redistribute wealth according to its fiscal and political interests and thus to encourage, discourage or prohibit different economic activities and agents'. Mercantilist bureaucracies increase rather than reduce the cost of transactions (De Soto 1989: 207). In Peru, as in Zaire, formal business has been gradually stifled by taxes and regulations and production has stagnated, but informal business openly defies the law. Cities are surrounded by migrant settlements, their streets are invaded by peddlars, beggars and thieves, and their markets are primarily supplied by smuggled or illegally manufactured goods (ibid: 221). 'Informal institutions and the protected space they have created now enable anyone to confront the mercantilist state instead of succumbing to it' (ibid: 232).

It is this aspect of the second economy that we have claimed has resulted in a change in the social structure and balance of power in Zairian society. No longer are the subordinated classes dependent on scarce jobs and the opportunities for rents that they may bring; other sources of income have proliferated as second economy enterprise has expanded. The defeat of the state in some areas of its oppression is evident in its inability to enforce regulations; it has opted out and simply ignores much of what is going on. This new economic base for the subordinated classes challenges the process whereby the dominant class has consolidated its position and attempted to close its boundaries. Through the second economy people are able to secure some sort of living, and in some cases enrich themselves. For those who have the money, this alternative society offers private education and medical services to replace the public ones that the state has allowed to decay, and which the members of the dominant class can afford to seek overseas. In this system, although the rich get richer, and the poor get poorer, some sort of transformation of society is in process. Opportunities that were not there before are opening up, since the dominant class cannot monopolize the second economy or control its expansion. How far this process can go, and its long-term-political implications, are still in question.

Notes

1. In January 1987 the official rate was 83 Z = 1 $ or 220 Z = 100 FB, but the parallel rate was 102-3 Z = 1 $ or 260-70 Z = 100 FB. Floating the zaire in the monetary reform of 1983 eliminated the parallel money market as long as the difference between the official rate and the parallel rate did not go over 10%, but after October 1985 the gap between the two rates began to widen; by the end of 1987 it was 30%.
2. These women may work on their own account, or on commission from other money changers or from businessmen who set them up.
3. Religious sects have proliferated outside the official churches in recent years.
4. Flour is milled at a flour mill in Matadi, but 30-48,000 tonnes are also imported annually from Europe; meanwhile about 10,000 tonnes are smuggled out of Bas Zaire (Flouriot, personal communication, April 1987). Rice is imported into western Zaire, at the same time as it is produced and smuggled out in the east.
5. In a study of 160 gold diggers south and east of Mbuji Mayi in 1983 and 1985, 38% were students or teachers (Tshibanza 1986: 345).

References

Appadurai, Arjun. 1986. *The Social Life of Things*. Cambridge: Cambridge University Press.

Baerhrel, Claude (with Tshimanga Nsata, Nsungani Ndengo, Pierre Yves Bellon, Christian Monnier). 1985. *Transports Informels à Kinshasa*. Kinshasa: Bureau d'Études d'Aménagement et d'Urbanisme (BEAU).

Basu, Kaushik. 1984. 'Implicit Interest Rates, Usury and Isolation in Backward Agriculture'. *Cambridge Journal of Economics* 8: 145–159.

Beach, D.N. 1983. 'The Zimbabwe Plateau and its Peoples'. In David Birmingham and Phyllis Martin (eds) *History of Central Africa*. Vol. 1. New York: Longman.

Beckman, Bjorn. 1987. 'Public Investment and Agrarian Transformation in Northern Nigeria'. In Michael Watts (ed) *State, Oil and Agriculture in Nigeria*. Institute of International Studies, University of California, Berkeley, pp. 110–137.

——— 1988. 'Peasants and Democratic Struggles in Nigeria'. *Review of African Political Economy* 41: 30–44.

BEAU. 1986. 'Consommation des Produits Vivriers à Kinshasa'. Kinshasa.

Bernard, Guy. 1972. 'Conjugalité et Rôle de la Femme à Kinshasa'. *Canadian Journal of African Studies* 6, 2: 261–274.

Bézy, Fernand, Jean-Philippe Peemans, Jean-Marie Wautelet. 1981. *Accumulation et Sous-Développement au Zaire, 1960–1980*. Louvain-la-Neuve: Presse Universitaire de Louvain.

Bhaduri, Amit. 1983. *The Economic Structure of Backward Agriculture*. London: Academic Press.

Biaya, T.K. 1985. 'La Cuistrerie de Mbuji Mayi (Zaire)'. *Génève Afrique* 23, 1: 62–85.

Blades, Derek W. 1982. 'The Hidden Economy and the National Accounts'. *OECD Economic Outlook*, Occasional Studies, no. 2, pp. 28–45.

Callaghy, Thomas M. 1984. *The State-Society Struggle: Zaire in Comparative Perspective*. New York: Columbia University Press.

CECOPANE. 1981–82. *Rapport de Recherche*. 4 vols.

——— 1982. *Mission au Zaire. Rapport*. 7.

Chazan, Naomi H. 1982. 'Development, Underdevelopment and the State in Ghana'. Working paper no. 8, Boston University African Studies Center.

Comhaire-Sylvain, Suzanne. 1968. *Femmes de Kinshasa Hier et Aujourd'hui*. Paris: Mouton.

Conjoncture Economique. 1984, 1985, 1987. Vols. 23, 24, 26. Kinshasa: Département de l'Économie Nationale, Industrie et Commerce.

De Soto, Hernando. 1989. *The Other Path: the Invisible Revolution in the Third World*. New York: Harper and Row.

Delis, Philippe and Christian Girard. 1985. 'Gestion Foncière Populaire par la Construction en Dur à Kinshasa'. *Les Annales de la Recherche Urbaine*.

Dickerman, Carol. 1984. 'City Women and the Colonial Regime: Usumbura 1939–1962'. *African Urban Studies* 18 (Spring): 33–48.

Economist Intelligence Unit. 1989. *Zaire, Country Profile 1988–1989*. London: The Economist.

Fassin, D. 1986. 'La Vente Illicite des Médicaments au Sénégal: Économies 'Parallèles', État et Société'. *Politique Africaine* 23: 123–130.

Feige, Edgar L. 1979. 'How Big is the Irregular Economy?' *Challenge*. November–December.

Flouriot, Jean. 1986. 'Zaire: La Dépendance Vivrière des Grandes Villes: Lubumbashi et Kinshasa, Évolution Récente'. Kinshasa: BEAU. Consultant's Report, February.

Fodouop, Kengne. 1988. 'La Contrebande entre le Cameroun et le Nigeria'. *Les Cahiers d'Outre-Mer* 161: 5–26.

Gershuny, J.I. and R.E. Pahl. 1980. 'Britain in the Decade of the Three Economies'. *New Society* 51, 900: 7–9.

Gould, Terri. 1978. 'Value Conflict and Development: The Struggle of the Professional Zairian Woman'. *Journal of Modern African Studies* 16 (March): 133–140.

Gouvernorat du Kivu. 1985a. *Étude des Collectivités Rurales. Géographie, Démographie, Économie.* Bukavu, Kivu.

——— 1985b. *Productions Vivriers. Campagne 1984–85.* Bukavu, Kivu.

Green, Reginald H. 1981. '*Magendo* in the Political Economy of Uganda: Pathology, Parallel System or Dominant Sub-Mode of Production?' Discussion Paper 64, Institute of Development Studies, University of Sussex.

Guyer, Jane. 1986. 'Intra-Household Processes and Farming Systems Research: Perspectives from Anthropology'. In Joyce L. Mook (ed.) *Understanding Africa's Rural Households and Farming Systems*, Boulder, Colorado: Westview.

Hart, Keith. 1973. 'Informal Income Opportunities and Urban Employment in Ghana'. *Journal of Modern African Studies* 11, 1: 61–89.

——— 1985. 'The Informal Economy'. *Cambridge Anthropology* 10, 2: 54–59.

Henn, Jean, Diane Russell et al. 1988. Mission-Wide Evaluation of Women in Development. USAID/Zaire, October.

Hill, Polly. 1986. *Development Economics on Trial: the Anthropological Case for the Prosecution.* Cambridge: Cambridge University Press.

Houyoux, Joseph. 1973. *Budgets Ménagers, Nutrition et Mode de Vie à Kinshasa.* Kinshasa: Presses Universitaires du Zaire.

Houyoux, Joseph and Kinavwuidi Niwembo. 1986. *Kinshasa 1975.* Kinshasa: BEAU.

Houyoux, Joseph, Kinavwuidi Niwembo and Okita Onya. 1986. *Budgets des Ménages, Kinshasa 1986.* Kinshasa: BEAU.

Igue Ogunsola J. 1976. 'Un Aspect des Échanges entre le Dahomey et le Nigeria: le Commerce du Cacao'. *Bulletin de l'IFAN* T.38, série B. no. 3, pp. 636–669.

——— 1977. 'Le Commerce de Contrebande et les Problèmes Monétaires en Afrique Occidentale'. Cotonou: CEFAP.

——— 1983. 'L'Officiel, le parallèle et le Clandestin'. *Politique Africaine* 9: 29–51.

——— 1985. 'Rente Petrolière et Commerce des Produits Agricoles à la Périphérie du Nigeria: les Cas du Benin et du Niger'. Montpellier: INRA/ESR.

Jagannathan, N. Vijay. 1987. *Informal Markets in Developing Countries.* Oxford: Oxford University Press.

Jeffries, Richard. 1982. 'Rawlings and the Political Economy of Underdevelopment in Ghana'. *African Affairs* 81, 324.

Jurion, F. and J. Henry. 1967. *De l'Agriculture Itinérante à l'Agriculture Intensifiée.* Brussels: INEAC.

Karuhije Mbonimba. 1985. 'Poussée des Maisons Commerciales à Mbuji-Mayi'. *UJUVI* (ISP-Bunia) 6: 175–193.

Kasay Katsuva, L.L. 1983. *Le Pays Nande au Kivu Septentrional (Zaire): Dynamisme des Populations et Organisation de l'Espace en Milieu Equatorial d'Altitude.* Mémoire, Université de Lubumbashi.

Kisangani, Emizet. 1985. 'A Social Dilemma in a Less Developed Country: the Massacre of the African Elephant in Zaire'. National Research Council, Proceedings of the conference on Common Property Resource Management, Annapolis, Maryland. Washington, D.C.: National Academy Press.

Kydd, Jonathan. 1988. 'Coffee After Copper? Structural Adjustment, Liberalisation and Agriculture in Zambia'. *Journal of Modern African Studies* 26, 2: 227–251.

LaFontaine, Jean. 1974. 'Free Women of Kinshasa'. In J. Davis (ed.) *Choice and Change: Essays in Honor of Audrey I. Richards.* Atlantic Highlands, New Jersey: Humanities Press.

Lambert, Denis-Clair. 1981. 'Les Inégalités de Revenus dans le Tiers Monde. Trois Correctifs: Démographie-Inflation Économie Souterraine'. *Revue Tiers Monde* 22, 88: 837–863.

Legum, Colin (ed). 1983–84. *Africa Contemporary Record*, vol. 16. Africana.

Leslie, Winsome J. 1987. *The World Bank and Structural Transformation in Developing Countries.* Boulder, Colorado: Lynne Rienner.

Lukusa, M. and Tshibanza, M. 1985. 'Déclin de Tshilenge: Conséquence d'une Politique de Développement Centré sur Mbuji-Mayi et de la Législation Préventive et Répressive de la Fraude des Diamants'. *UJUVI* (ISP-Bunia), 6: 111–136.

MacGaffey, Janet. 1987. *Entrepreneurs and Parasites: the Struggle for Indigenous Capitalism in Zaire*. Cambridge: Cambridge University Press.

———— 1988. 'Evading Male Control: Women in the Second Economy in Zaire'. In *Patriarchy and Class*, Sharon B. Stichter and Jane L. Parpart (eds). Boulder, Colorado: Westview Press.

———— 1991. 'Initiatives From Below: Zaire's "Other Path" to Social and Economic Restructuring'. In Goran Hyden and Michael Bratton (eds) *Governance and Politics in Africa: Perestroika without Glasnost?* Boulder, Colorado: Lynne Rienner.

Maliyamkono, T.L. and M.S.D. Bagachwa. 1990. *The Second Economy in Tanzania*. London: James Currey.

Marks, Shula. 1987. *Not Either an Experimental Doll: The Separate Worlds of Three South African Women*. Bloomington, Indiana: Indiana University Press.

Mateso Mande. 1985. 'La Fonction Commerciale dans la Ville de Bunia: Cas du Quartier Sukisa'. *UJUVI* (ISP-Bunia), 6: 159–173.

Mattera, Philip. 1985. *Off-the-Books: the Rise of the Underground Economy*. New York: St. Martin's Press.

Mkandawire, Thandika. 1986. 'The Informal Sector in the Labour Reserve Economies of Southern Africa With Special Reference to Zimbabwe'. *Africa Development* 11, 1: 61–82.

Mohsen Toumi. 1987. 'Circuits Officiels Réseaux Parallèles – les Echanges en Afrique'. *Science et Vie Economique*, 24: 45–57.

Momoh, Eddie. 1988. 'The Menace of Smuggling'. *West Africa* no. 3706. Aug. 22–28.

Morice, Alain. 1985. 'Commerce Parallèle et Troc à Luanda'. *Politique Africaine* 17: 105–120.

———— 1987. 'Guinée 1985: État, Corruption et Trafics'. *Les Temps Moderne* 42, 487: 108–136.

Moser, Caroline. 1978. 'Informal Sector or Petty Commodity Production: Dualism or Dependence in Urban Development?' *World Development* 9/10: 1041–64.

Mubake Mumeme. 1984. I. 'Crise, inflation et comportements individuels d'Adaption au Zaire: Solution ou Aggravation du Problème?' II. 'Économie Souterraine et Secteur Informel au Zaire: Caractéristiques et Fonctions'. *Zaire Afrique* 185: 263–72, 188: 491–97

Muyayalo, V.V. 1976. 'L'Economie Informelle dans une Zone de *Squatting* à Lubumbashi: Le Cas de Kigoma'. Lubumbashi: National University of Zaire: Department of Sociology-Anthropology, Mémoire.

Newbury, Catharine M. 1984. 'Dead and Buried or Just Underground? The Privatization of the State in Zaire'. In B. Jewsiewicki (ed.) *État Indépendant du Congo, Congo Belge, République Démocratique du Congo, République du Zaire?* Ste-Foy, Quebec: Editions SAFI Press.

Newbury, C. and B.G. Schoepf. 1989. 'State, Peasantry and Agrarian Crisis in Zaire: Does Gender Make a Difference?' In *Women and the State in Africa*, Jane L. Parpart and Kathleen A. Staudt, (eds.) Boulder, Colorado: Lynne Rienner, pp. 91–110.

Outer Circle Policy Unit. 1976. 'Policing the Hidden Economy: the Significance and Control of Fiddles.' London.

Pain, Marc. 1984. *Kinshasa: la Ville et la Cité*. Paris: eds. de l'ORSTOM.

Péan, Pierre. 1988. *L'Argent Noir: Corruption et Sous-Développement*. Paris: Fayard.

Portes, Alejandro and John Walton. 1981. *Labor, Class and the International System*. New York: Academic Press.

Prunier, G. 1983. 'Le Magendo: Essai sur quelques Aspects Marginaux des Échanges Commerciaux en Afrique Orientale'. *Politique Africaine* 9: 53–62.

Redclift, Nanneke and E. Mingione (eds). 1985. *Beyond Employment: Household, Gender and Subsistence*. Oxford: Basil Blackwell.

Roberts, B. 1988. 'The Informal Sector in Comparative Perspective'. Paper presented at the Meeting of the Society for Economic Anthropology, Knoxville, Tennessee.

Russell, Diane. 1989. 'The Outlook for Liberalization in Zaire: Evidence from Kisangani's Rice Trade'. Working Papers in African Studies, No. 139, Boston University.

Schatzberg, Michael G. 1980. *Politics and Class in Zaire: Bureaucracy, Business and Beer in Lisala*. New York: Africana.

———— 1988. *The Dialectics of Oppression in Zaire*. Bloomington, Indiana: Indiana University Press.

Schissel, Howard. 1989. 'Africa's Underground Economy'. *Africa Report*, Jan./Feb.: 43–46.

Schoepf, B.G. 1978/81. 'Women in the Informal Economy of Lubumbashi: The Case of the Ndumba'. Paper presented at the IV International Congress of African Studies, Kinshasa, December 1978 and in *Proceedings of the 1981 Annual Meeting of the (US) Association of African Studies*.

———— 1984. 'Man and Biosphere in Zaire', In *The Politics of Agriculture in Tropical Africa*. Jonathan Barker, (ed.) Beverly Hills: Sage Publishers, pp. 269–290.

———— 1985a. 'Food Crisis and Class Formation: An Example from Shaba', *Review of African Political Economy*, No. 33, August: 33–43.

———— 1985b. 'Priorité des Priorités', Zaire African Food Systems Initiative Assessment Team Report, pp. 11–35. Washington, D.C.: US Peace Corps, April.

———— 1986. 'Current Political Economy of Burundi, Madagascar, Rwanda and Zaire'. In *Collier's Encyclopedia Yearbook*, pp. 158, 305, 438-39, 570–571. Reprinted in *Merit Students' Encyclopedia* and *Funk and Wagnall's New Encyclopedia Yearbook*. New York: Macmillan.

———— 1987. 'Social Structure, Women's Status and Sex Differential Nutrition in the Zairian Copperbelt', *Urban Anthropology* 16,1 (Spring): 73–102.

———— 1988. 'Women, AIDS and Economic Crisis in Central Africa'. *Canadian Journal of African Studies* 22, 3: 625–644.

———— 1989a. 'At Risk for AIDS: Women's Lives in Zaire'. Colloquium, Murray Research Center, Radcliffe College, December 12.

———— 1989b. 'The Social Production of Heterosexual AIDS in Zaire'. Colloquium, The Bunting Institute, Radcliffe College, December 13.

———— 1990. 'Theory and Practice in Anthropological Research with African Women: Case Studies from Zaire'. Paper prepared for Wenner Gren Symposium, no. 111 on AIDS Research: Issues for Anthropological Theory, Method and Practice. Estes Park, Colorado, June 25–July 1.

———— in press. 'Knowledge of Women, Women's Knowledge: Texts of "Tradition" and "Modernity" in Zaire'. Forthcoming in B. Jewsiewicki (ed.) *The Transfer of Knowledge from Europe to Africa*.

Schoepf, Brooke G., and Claude Schoepf. 1981. 'Zaire's Rural Development in Perspective'. In Brooke G. Schoepf, (ed.) *The Role of U.S. Universities in International Rural and Agricultural Development*, pp. 243–257. Tuskegee Institute, Center for Rural Development.

———— 1984. 'Peasants, Capitalists and the State in the Lufira Valley'. *Canadian Journal of African Studies* 18, 1: 89–93.

———— and Claude Schoepf. 1987. 'Food Crisis and Agrarian Change in the Eastern Highlands of Zaire'. *Urban Anthropology* 16, 1 (Spring): 5–37.

Schoepf, B.G., Walu Engundu, Rukarangira wa Nkera, Payanzo Ntsomo and Claude Schoepf. In press (a). 'Action Research on AIDS with Women in Kinshasa'. *Social Science and Medicine* and Meredeth Turshen (ed.) *Women and Health in Africa*. New York: Africa World Press.

Schoepf, B.G., Walu Engundu, C. Schoepf and D. Russell. 1990. 'Women and Structural Adjustment in Zaire: The Impact of Market Forces'. In C. Gladwin, (ed.) *African Women Farmers*. Gainesville: University of Florida Press.

Schoepf, Brooke G. and Walu Engundu. 1987. 'Women's Survival Strategies: AIDS and the Deepening Economic Crisis in Zaire'. Colloquia, Boston University and Columbia University, Center for African Studies, December.

Schwartz, Alf. 1972. 'Illusion d'une Émancipation et Aliénation Réelle de l'Ouvrière Zairoise'. *Canadian Journal of African Studies* 6, 2: 183–212.

Seibel, Hans Dieter and Michael T. Marx. 1987. *Dual Financial Markets in Africa: Case Studies of Linkages between Informal and Formal Financial Institutions*. Saarbrücken, Fort Lauderdale: Breitenbach Publishers.

Smith, J.D. 1985. 'Market Motives in the Informal Economy'. In G. Gaertner and A. Wenig (eds.) *The Economics of the Shadow Economy*. Heidelberg: Springer, pp. 161–177.

Szelenyi, Ivan (in collaboration with Robert Manchin, Pal Juhasz, Balint Magyar, and Bill Martin). 1988. *Socialist Entrepreneurs: Embourgeoisement in Rural Hungary*. Madison: University of Wisconsin Press.

Tripp, Ali M. 1988. 'Defending the Right to Subsist: the State vs. the Urban Informal Economy in Tanzania'. Paper presented to the Meeting of the African Studies Association, Chicago, Illinois.

Tshibanza Monji. 1986. 'Le Phenomène Creuseurs et ses Paradoxes'. *Zaire Afrique* 206: 341–354.

Tshibanza Monji and Tshimanga Mulangula. 1985. 'Matières Précieuses et Libéralisation: Esquisse d'un Bilan Provisoire'. *Zaire Afrique* 196: 337–47.

Vwakyanakazi Mukohya. 1982. *African Traders in Butembo, Eastern Zaire (1960–1980): a Case Study of Informal Entrepreneurship in a Cultural Context of Central Africa*. Ph.D. Dissertation, Madison: University of Wisconsin.

———— 1982. 'Traders in Butembo Revisited: Further Reflections on the Second Economy in Zaire'. Paper presented at the African Studies Association Meetings, Madison, Wisconsin.

Wiles, Peter. 1987. 'The Second Economy, its Definitional Problems'. In Sergio Alessandrini and Bruno Dallago (eds.) *The Unofficial Economy*. Aldershot: Gower, pp. 21–33.

Wilson, F.R. 1982. 'Reinventing the Past and Circumscribing the Future: *Authenticité* and the Negative

Image of Women's Work in Zaire'. In Edna G. Bay (ed.) *Women and Work in Africa*, pp. 153–170. Boulder, Colorado: Westview.

Witte, Anne D. 1987. 'The Nature and Extent of Unrecorded Activity: a Survey Concentrating on Recent US Research'. In Sergio Alessandrini and Bruno Dallago (eds.) *The Unofficial Economy*. Aldershot: Gower, pp. 61–81.

Wolf, Eric. 1966. 'Kinship, Friendship and Patron-Client Relations in Complex Societies'. In Michael Banton (ed.) *The Social Anthropology of Complex Societies*. Cambridge: Cambridge University Press.

World Bank. 1989. *Sub-Saharan Africa: From Crisis to Sustainable Growth. A Long-Term Perspective Study*. Washington, DC.

Young, M.Crawford. 1965. *Politics in the Congo*. Princeton, New Jersey: Princeton University Press.

—— 1984. 'Zaire: Is There a State?' In B. Jewsiewicki (ed.) *État Indépendant du Congo, Congo Belge, République Démocratique du Congo, République du Zaire?* Ste-Foy, Quebec: Editions SAFI Press.

Young, Crawford, and Thomas Turner. 1985. *The Rise and Decline of the Zairian State*. Madison: University of Wisconsin Press.

MOUVEMENT POPULAIRE DE LA REVOLUTION

REPUBLIQUE DU ZAIRE

ZONE DE LUOZI
COLLECTIVITE DE KINKENGE.

LARGE DIFFUSION
LUZAISU KWA NKANGU MU ZI GROUPEMENTS KINKENGE-LUANGU-
Communiqué destiné à la population des groupements de LUWALA NTEKOLO A
BILEKUA BITUVUIDI (Produits agricoles). *Kinkenge-Luangu-et Luala vente de nos produits.*

1. NTUTU WA MAFUTA	10 ZAIRES	SANGALA KIA MAFUTA	140 Z
		KITADI	70 Z
2. NTUTU WA MALAVU LUNGUILA	3 ZAIRES	SANGALA LUNGUILA	30 Z
WENA YE NKANDA WA LETA	4 Z	SANGALA LUNGUILA	40 Z
3. NTUTU WA NSAMBA	4 Z	SANGALA LUNGUILA	40 Z
YENA YE NKANDA WA LETA	5 Z	SANGALA LUNGUILA	50 Z
4. MADEZO MU VELA	5 Z	–	–
5. NGUBA MU VELA	4 Z	NSAKU YA NGUBA	400 Z
6. KUNKU KIA FUFU BASU BI (4)	2 Z	NSAKU YA FUFU	300 Z
7. VELA YA LOSO	3 Z	NSAKU YA LOSO	300 Z
8. MBIZI YA NGOMBE	–	1 KGR 1 KILO	50 Z
9. MBIZI YA BUALA EVO YA MFINDA	–	1 KILO	40 Z
10. MBIZI YA MBALA	–	BULU KIA MVIMBA	60 à 70Z
11. NSIBIZI YA MVIMBA	100 Z	YA INENE	120 Z
12. NGONDO YA MFINDA/NSENGI	100 Z	YA INENE	140 Z
13. NSUSU NKENTO VO MBAKALA	50 Z	YA INENE	60 Z
14. BULU KIA WAYI	50 Z	YA INENE	50 Z
15. KUANGA	2 Z	KIA KINENE	5 Z
16. MASANGU MA YUMA/MA NLANGU (4)	2 Z	MA MANENE (3) TATU	2 Z

N.B. WONSO UNA LEMBUA LANDA NTALU ZAZI UNAFUTA NSIKU WAUNENE
KUA LUYALU. Celui ou celle qui ne respectera pas ces prix payera une amende à la
Collectivité.

Fait à Kinkenge, Le 27 Février 1985
LE PRESIDENT DU COMITE POPULAIRE COLL.
CHEF DE COLLECTIVITE.

Appendix 2: Average Prices for Agricultural Products and Small Livestock in Villages and Markets in Luozi Zone and in Kinshasa April 1987 (in zaires)

Product	Unit	Average Price In Luozi Zone	Price in Kinshasa	% Mark-up
Manioc pudding	.5 kg.	10.3	30	191
Manioc tubers	1 basin	253.0	750	196
Manioc leaves	1 bunch	1.75	10	471
Shelled peanuts	1 glass	8.5	35	311
Unshelled peanuts	1 heap	3.5	5	42.8
Beans	1 glass	11.3	30	165
Fresh tomatoes	100 g. pile	3.8	10	163
Peppers	100 g. pile	4.2	10	138
Vegetables	1 bunch	3.5	10	185
Palm oil	.75 l.	22.7	40	76.2
Bananas	3	3.5	10	185
Avocados	1 pile	4.5	25	455
Safous	1 pile	4.0	20	400
Oranges	350 g.	3.8	10	185
Chicken	1	178.0	300	68.5
Duck	1	400.0	600	50
Goat	1	1,433.0	1,900	32.6
Pineapple	1	10.0	80	700
Sugar cane	1	10.0	10	0
Local rice	1 glass	8.2	10	21.9
Eggplant	1 pile	5	10	100

Index

174

Tripp, A.M. 16, 39–40n.
Tshibanza, M. 25n. 63, 155, 158n.

Uganda 15, 16, 50, 54, 63, 64
unemployment 9, 75, 76, 149
Upper Zaire 31, 54, 57, 58, 59, 68, 152

vehicles 54, 61, 64, 65, 80, 83, 87, 90,
    106
  stolen 84–87

wages and salaries 9, 13–16 pass. 24, 28,
    35, 36–37, 38, 78, 107, 124, 125,
    126–130 pass. 135–144 pass. 149, 154
Weber, M. 8, 153

Wiles, P. 12
Wilson, F.R. 150n.
Witte, A. 12, 157
World Bank 2, 10, 21, 24, 151n. 156
Wolf, E. 30

Young, C. 17, 24n. 27, 39, 151n.
youth 65–66, 68, 86
  in gold mining 50
  in smuggling 23, 47, 54

Zairianization 28, 70n.
Zambia 16, 23, 24, 72, 75–81, 84
  vehicles 84–87